FAMILY MANAGEMENT

a guide

against

PARENTAL FAILURE

ISAAC ARIGBEDE

(C) 2016 I.O. Arigbede

All rights reserved. No part of this publication may be reproduced, stored in a retrieval system or transmitted in any form or by any means without the prior permission of the author.

Printed by: AROLIS SERVICES,

3, Sewage Avenue,

Behind Jakande Estate,

Abesan, Ipaja,

Lagos State.

Phone: 07032550987, 07012987048.

PREFACE

"FAMILY MANAGEMENT: A Guide Against Parental Failure" is an ideal handbook for the family and for those preparing for marriage. It is completely different from the other family-related books in terms of its valuable benefits. The benefits include but not limited to the moral and the logical practical approaches to preventing or correcting differences with a view to having a successful marriage and a happy family relationship.

This book has three different parts namely, the introduction, the pre-marital period and the marital period. The first part which is the introduction chapter highlights the family composition and trends. The second part, chapter two to chapter five cover the personal requirements for adults who are preparing for marriage. These requirements are treated under virtues for marital success, courtship, compatibility, and marriage; family planning and management and so on. Finally, the third part, chapter six to chapter twenty three focus on preparing and caring for baby, combined roles of the family, need for home training, moral principles, sex education, drug addiction and caring for ageing parents just to mention a few.

This book has a total of one hundred and twenty four pages.

ACKNOWLEDGEMENT

This book has been made possible by the special grace of God Almighty who directed and guided me. I greatly appreciate the priceless gift of good health, precious time for this intensive research work, knowledge and wisdom God gave me in completing this work. I remain ever grateful to Almighty God.

I will also like to express my sincere appreciation to family and friends who contributed greatly to the successful completion of this book.

CONTENTS

	Pages
Preface	iii
Acknowledgement	iv

INTRODUCTION

1. Family Composition and Trends — 1–3

SECTION 1: PRE-MARITAL PERIOD

2. Virtues for Marital Success — 4 – 9
3. Courtship, Compatibility and Marriage — 10 – 16
4. The Need for Family Planning and Management — 17 – 23
5. Secret of Marriage Happiness — 24 – 27

SECTION 2: MARITAL PERIOD

6. Preparing and Caring for Baby — 28 – 32
7. Combined Roles of the Family — 33 – 40
8. Responsibilities of Children — 41 – 47
9. Teach Children Good Home Training — 48 – 52
10. The Need for Qualitative Education and Skills — 53 – 60
11. Sound Moral Principles and Values — 61 – 65

12. Managing Grown-up Children	66 – 72
13. Sex Education	73 – 77
14. Drug Addiction	78 – 79
15. A Balanced View of Alcoholic Drinks	80 – 82
16. Dressing and Hair Styles	83 – 85
17. Prostitution	86 – 89
18. Selfishness, Greed and Corruption	90 – 93
19. Choose Good Companions	94 – 97
20. Maintain a Balanced View of Recreation	98 – 101
21. Teach Children Home Management	102 – 105
22. Family Relationship Management Virtues	106 – 116
23. Care for Ageing Parents	117 – 122
Summary	123 – 124

INTRODUCTION

CHAPTER 1

FAMILY COMPOSITION AND TRENDS

Family can be defined as a group consisting of the father, the mother and their children. The parents which make up the building block of the family institution extend beyond tribe, religion and geographical location. It cuts across the local, the national and international boundaries. Family is the oldest and widest institution on earth and it plays a vital role in human society throughout history. The family is the divine arrangement for bringing up children. In many ways, it is the most important. It is society's most basic unit.

Research findings show that; an entire civilization have survived or disappeared, depending on whether family life was strong or weak. In agreement with this fact, the family is the nucleus of every society, every nation and by extension, it is the core or central part of the entire world of mankind. Therefore, the prevailing conditions in the family determine human behavior in the society, in the nation and in the world as a whole.

Human society feels only as good as its family. History shows that as the family arrangement erodes, the strength of communities and nations weakens. When moral decay destroyed families in ancient powerful nations, their civilization disintegrated, making them vulnerable to conquest by their enemies who had a well managed, morally stable and strong family bond. The family arrangement offers a happy and pleasant home to all. Yes, the family is a human necessity. It has a direct effect on the stability of the society and the well being of children and future generations.

There is no gain saying the fact that the picture of the family situation worldwide is not attractive. Many factors have contributed and still causing the downfall of the family institution. Some of the causes of family downfall or family breakdown include but not limited to harsh economic situation resulting in financial problem in the family. Also, drug and alcohol are contributing to family breakdown. Single parent family have resulted in many family breakdowns, family with unmarried parents have resulted in many breakdowns, complete lack of family plan or unrealistic family plan, early marriage, loss of job, pay cut, health and behavioral incompatibility among couples, gambling and so forth.

It is a vogue to divorce and marry another person just to have a change of partner nowadays. Some see divorce as a means of freedom from family stress, control or responsibility. Growing numbers prefer to live together without being legally married or without the responsibilities of marriage (cohabitation). These are part of global trends and they continue to have adverse effects on the family.

When the foundation (**parents**) is weak, the structure (**children**) is bound to collapse. This is a vivid description of the bad consequences of failure in the family. Some of these bad outcomes include; homeless children, rapist, terrorists, robbers, assassins, drug addicts and so on. Many are escapees from broken homes and some are cast out by families that can no longer support them. It is crystal clear that the family is in a serious crisis. For example; spousal violence, drug abuse, excessive use of alcohol, child abuse, teenage rebellion, crimes and other problems continue to dominate in many families globally. True, broken families and dissolution are not new in history. But family bonds have never been weaker than in the 20th century. In addition, a more general cause is that the basic attitude toward marriage and family life has changed radically.

Many families have turned to different sources for lasting solution. Some of these sources include; marriage counselors, academics, marriage celebrants, personal beliefs and even fortune tellers. But not all these sources are successful in preventing marriage and family relationship breakdown. What important **pre-marital** and **marital** personal and combined actions, behaviors and decisions should prospective couples and families make respectively?

SECTION 1

PRE-MARITAL PERIOD

CHAPTER 2

VIRTUES FOR MARITAL SUCCESS

The family institution is all encompassing and therefore should be given a very serious consideration. There is need for deep sense of responsibility and devotion to one's future spouse, children and parents. These essential qualities must be developed or enhanced by would-be couples because these will form the solid foundation for their marriage and family success. Marital successes will not just happen, it requires understanding.

Understanding here means seeking to please each other, freely admitting faults, doing things together, keeping romance alive, freely forgiving, being united in raising and disciplining of children, not neglecting family interest for unimportant activities, good money and time management and so on. For long lasting peace and harmony, some important qualities must be developed by prospective couples before thinking about marriage. What are some of these qualities? How are they relevant in marital relationship?

These important virtues among others include love, joy, peace, long suffering, kindness, goodness, faith, mildness, self-control and so on. These virtues will make it possible for spouse and family to enjoy peaceful relationship and happiness.

LOVE

A person can be said to manifest love if he or she does not brag, not get puffed up, not boast on what has been achieved or what will be done. The person should not seek or expect the applause and admiration of people and should not push another person down to make himself or herself appear greater. This person should rejoice with people who achieve greater responsibility instead of hurtful jealousy. Also, a loving person is expected to behave decently, put up with the unfavorable conditions and wrong actions of others with a good purpose, avoid rudeness and be respectful.

A loving person cares for others, not unnecessarily become provoked, shows concern for others, does not insist that everything be done in his or her own way alone, seeks the advantage of the others, does not look for an occasion or an excuse for provocation, not moved to outburst of anger, not easily offended by what others say or do, does not suspect or disbelieve others unless there was absolute proof. Furthermore, a loving person has faith in others but not gullible and not keeping account of injury for future revenge. Also, loving person supports righteousness and justice and does not take side sentimentally with wrongdoers.

Also, any person who wants the good attributes of love to reflect in his or her behavior should be able to bear things, hopeful, enduring and optimistic. In other words, the person should be ready to overlook an offence if it not too serious and privately point out an offence to the wrongdoer with the aim of forgiveness and continue to build up stronger and expect a change of situation for positive outcomes.

JOY

True joy is a quality of the heart and can reflect the whole body for good. Joy is the emotion excited by the acquisition or expectation of good; it is a state of happiness or exultation. The world is endowed with many good things that mankind will enjoy. One of these is marriage; therefore marriage was originated to be a joyful union for family development.

PEACE

This is another virtue expected of every mankind. It is a state of being free from disturbance. It can convey the idea of good health, safety, soundness, welfare, well-being, or absence of conflict. Those who desire to seek and pursue peace must turn away from what is bad and do what is good. Couple can enjoy long lasting peace if a precious relationship is developed between each other.

LONG-SUFFERING

Long-suffering means slow to anger. It is the patient endurance of wrong or provocation, combined with a refusal to give up hope for improvement in the disturbed relationship. Long-suffering therefore has a purpose, looking particularly to the welfare of the one causing the disagreeable situation. It does not mean the condoning of wrong. It ends with good to those causing provocation. Ending long-suffering with good in most cases is recommended.

KINDNESS

This involves showing affection to others. It is the quality or state of taking an active interest in the welfare of others. It also means extending friendly and helpful acts or favor. This is also a vital quality as it moves one to forgive another easily and freely. It is an act that preserves or promotes life. It is intervention on behalf of someone suffering misfortune or distress. It is a demonstration of friendship. It is a factor that brings relief from trouble. It is an expression of mercy. Kindness enable people to draw close to one another, strengthens peace and enhance friendship.

GOODNESS

This is a positive quality. It expresses itself in the performance of good and beneficial acts towards others. Goodness combines other qualities such as loving kindness, mercy and truth but does not condone or cooperate in any way with badness. It is also the quality or state of being good, showing moral excellence or virtue. Furthermore, it is the bestowing of beneficial things upon others and it is possible to cultivate goodness by being obedient.

FAITH

There is need for strong faith in each other. Faith is the basis for hope and the evidence for conviction concerning unseen realities. Faith is also the assured expectation of things hoped for, the evident demonstration of realities though not behold. It is an expression of confidence, trust and firm persuasion. Faith is not static, it grows. Therefore, those planning to marry and raise children should let faith grow in them. This will enable them have confidence in each other, trust each other and be convinced that both are faithful in their dealings. The overall positive effect of this quality is a reliable and trustworthy companionship and family.

MILDNESS

Mildness is synonymous with greatness, meekness and calmness. Mildness is not weakness but a manifestation of maturity and reasonableness in action. It is the tendency not to show a rebellious spirit when corrected by someone in a superior position. A mild or calm person by his quality, try as much as possible to avoid further anger in already tensed situation. It helps in improving one's personality by keeping down temper. It prevents extension of minor issues or problems to a regrettable end. A mild person is a humble person.

SELF-CONTROL

It is the ability to remain calm and not show your emotions even though you are feeling very angry, excited and so on. It is keeping in check, restraining or controlling one's actions, speeches or thought. It is a reflection of one's mind to avoid evil or condemn bad thoughts completely. There is need for self-control in the family. Failure to exercise self-control in a given situation can spoil someone's good record and lead into all kinds of difficulties. In addition, it allows faithfulness to flow freely in the family.

Although, perfect behavior is not expected from any member of the family, the need for peaceful co-existence and pleasant conduct is very important. These and many more positive results can be achieved by earnestly seeking and emulating the qualities discussed. In addition, these virtues are important in guiding every person and families in developing an excellent perspective about issues and acting wisely. Having a mindset of these invaluable qualities will be most rewarding for each and every person and particularly the spouse and the family.

CHAPTER 3

COURTSHIP, COMPATIBILITY AND MARRIAGE

COURTSHIP

Before a man and a woman get married, there is a period of assessment and/or getting to know each other. The time (weeks, months or years) when a single man and a single woman develop and maintain a serious and genuine close (non-sexual) relationship or observation prior to expression of interest or proposal in each other is called courtship. What are some of the benefits that can be derived from decent courtship? What are some of the cautions needed to keep courtship decent?

Courtship can be very beneficial if the foundation is based on honesty. That is both courting persons should disclose correct information and display genuine behavior for each other. Both parties should not camouflage their real personality so as to win each other's interest at all cost. This could ruin the marriage in future, with great regrets and sadness. Happy and successful marriage is the result of decent courtship.

Sincere and decent courtship can provide an opportunity to become better acquainted with the person whom you are considering spending the rest of your life. It is possible to learn each other's likes and dislikes, standards, habits and outlooks. Disposition, temper and reactions to problems or difficulties can also be identified. Courtship also makes it possible to observe vital qualities such as kindness, self-control, goodness, love, humility, money management and more qualities in each other.

In most cases and in most places, a man initiates courtship by expressing interest in a woman. But both of them need to be very careful if decent courtship is to be maintained. If courtship is a series of passionate expressions with little or no restraints, this will adversely affect the prospects for a successful marriage. For example, excessive physical contact will enhance sexual attraction for each other. In view of its possible negative outcome, it is advisable to limit each other very strictly as to physical contact during courtship. There is need for caution too in avoiding situations and appearances that can lead to expression of passion. These include lonely places, dark areas, indecent dressing, indecent jokes, immoral entertainments, and recreations and so on and so forth. However, wholesome courtship can be achieved when both parties engage in decent, balanced and appropriate activities.

Courtship could either be successful or unsuccessful depending on many factors that can be attributed to both courting persons. Successful courtship means the relationship can continue. If courtship is not successful, the relationship should stop. For example, if serious differences exist, the man and the woman should not fool each other into thinking that marriage will automatically solve the identified problems. It is necessary for the man and woman to sincerely ask the personal question; how well suited am I for the man or the woman?

COMPATIBILITY

If two people are compatible, they can have a good relationship because they have similar ideas, interests, goals, behaviors and so on. In general, compatibility is the ability of people to live together without problems. But perfect compatibility can never be attained by any person or group of persons. This is due to the fact that no human is perfect. Therefore, because of human imperfection, compatibility can be re-defined as the ability of people to live together with reduced problems. This implies that hundred percent performances in human activity should not be expected among prospective couples, married couples and the family as a whole.

Prospective couples should not be self-centered. Instead, both should seek mutual sources of happiness and be in tune with each other to enjoy long-lasting relationship. Many marriages end up in divorce due to incompatibility. If two persons are not well suited as a team, the going can be difficult. In other words, when couples have many different interests, goals, behavior and few things in common, the marital link might break. Also, for a truly successful marriage, couples must be good friends and enjoy each other's company. Therefore, they need to have many interests in common to be compatible. What other matters are relevant here?

Compatibility is not complete when very serious

primary issues such as family background, hereditary matters, health matters are not taken into consideration. For example, it is a must for prospective couples to consult medical personnel for blood group and genotype tests, HIV/AIDS, Diabetes, STDs (sexually transmitted diseases such as herpes, syphilis, gonorrhea, etc) and other blood and non-blood related diseases as well as infectious and non-infectious diseases such as tuberculosis. These right steps will prevent costly and terminal health problems in future. The medical personnel handling this part should be honest and frank in disclosing medical tests results. And these results must be disclosed to both courting couples at the same time.

Other vital reasons for medical tests are; to enable prospective couples have healthy children, to avoid a situation of childlessness, to avoid divorce in future and also to save money, time and other precious resources. What should be of greatest concern to prospective couples is their willingness to accept and abide with the blood screening results. That is, if the results are compatible, they can marry each other but if the results are not compatible, they must not marry each other.

In making final decision to marry, parents should allow their children to select their future spouse. The very important contributions of parents are to advice, to guide, to monitor and perhaps make objective assessment of their children's future spouse. Parents are expected to offer genuine assistance devoid of sentiments of any kind. It is equally vital for parents to be reasonably flexible rather than being coercive or unnecessarily rigid on minor issues that can be ignored without any serious outcomes.

MARRIAGE

Marriage is one of the most serious steps that one takes in life, so it should never be taken lightly. This is because it requires a life-long commitment to another person. It means a sharing of one's entire life with that person. Therefore, mature judgement is needed if that commitment is to be sound. Marriage is much more than joining together of two different personalities, two different families, two culturally different persons or two people with different beliefs. What then is marriage?

This is a legal relationship between a husband and a wife. It is the union of a man and a woman as husband and wife. Marriage is a divine institution authorized and set up by God. Marriage was designed to form a permanent bond of union between a man and a woman that they might be mutually helpful to each other. The basic purpose of marriage is to produce children. Therefore, marriage brings into existence the family unit. Marriage is an arrangement which affects both parents of the bride and the bridegroom. Although, both parents are affected by the marital relationship of their children, they should not interfere in their marital affairs. However, parents can intervene if invited or if situation urgently require their attention.

Wedding ceremonies last for a few days but marital

relationship is lifetime. Subsequent to wedding, the newly married couples will have to settle down as a new family unit in a new environment with almost everything completely new and changed. After the delight and merriment come the reality and the daily routine of life! These include getting up early, going to work, shopping and cooking meals, washing plates, cleaning the house and so on. These are facts of life. In other words, schedules are new, work may be new, budgets are made and there are additional new friends and in-laws to acquaint with.

The couple should always show maturity and realize that neither of them has the whole time and energy for himself or herself alone as it used to be before marriage. Now is time to show flexibility and accept the deeply satisfying responsibility of making marriage work. Not only are a man and a woman made differently, they also feel differently. So, consideration for the woman's need for tenderness is important. The husband should always express appreciation for the wife's contribution. Similarly, the wife should always help and complement her husband's efforts.

Therefore, the success of the marriage and happiness depend among other factors upon the willingness of the couples to adapt and adjust reasonably to suit prevailing situation. It is obvious that whole soul commitment is unavoidable. Therefore, commitment should not frighten couples and should not be seen as a burden. Instead, it should be seen as a source of security. This understanding of commitment should make couple want to stay together through 'thick and thin'. An appropriate suggestion for every single male and female is not to rush into marriage. Parents should not allow early marriage for their children. This is vital because the years spent living as a single decent adult (male or female) will result in precious experience that will make for more matured person and better qualified to be a suitable spouse.

CHAPTER 4

THE NEED FOR FAMILY PLANNING AND MANAGEMENT

These twin subjects are either treated carelessly or not given any attention by many families. Why is family planning and management important? The importance of these subjects will be discussed under four different categories namely; reasons for family planning, reasons for family management, family income management and time management and safety precaution.

REASONS FOR FAMILY PLANNING

Family planning is more than keeping money aside for wedding materials and ceremonies, it is not about getting one's choice of wife or husband, it is not about getting married to the man or woman of your choice. Family planning is more than just having children as an evidence of parenthood; it is even more than spending money judiciously. It is not just about spacing children. What other matters are involved in family planning?

In addition to the common objectives stated earlier, it is vital to compare the cost and benefits of getting married. It is very important for parents to create time and manage the time wisely with their children, to allow regular family discussions, to inculcate the proper moral or behavioral values in children and to set good examples for children. Also of importance is good resource planning such as financial or family income allocation for domestic needs, children's education and other vital matters. The application of these factors will set a solid foundation and prevent marriage or family from collapse.

Planning is a strategic course of action. Plan is a set of things to be done in order to achieve some objectives. Planning involves anticipation of the future course of events and therefore, bears an element of uncertainty in respect to its success. As a way of reducing the effects of uncertainty (e.g. economic problem and loss of job), planning as a mental process requires the use of imagination, intellectual faculties, foresight, sound judgement and so on. From this perspective, family planning therefore, is a set of actions and activities that a spouse intends to execute with a view to achieving marital success. Family plans must be flexible and contain achievable or realizable objectives.

A reasonable plan, free from fantasy world is a vital tool for successful marriage. In conformity with a practicable plan, would-be couples need to assess themselves objectively. This self assessment will enable prospective couples know themselves properly. There are some other vital factors that should be considered when planning for marriage.

Self assessment is a vital tool for would-be couples. Questions are good instruments for self assessment. It helps in knowing and discovering motives. The use of this tool will help those contemplating marriage to have a realistic view of both the cost and benefits of being married both in the short and long time.

In conclusion, a well prepared plan is characterized by setting achievable objectives, setting and implementing strategies, tactics and actions needed to achieve the objectives. Planning is the first thing couples must do.

REASONS FOR FAMILY MANAGEMENT

Every successful family management must have a solid family plan foundation. Family planning is an integral part of sound family management. A well-functioning family does not just happen. It requires some effort and time. Family management is the total responsibility of parents in implementing the family plans. Family management practices include preparation for children's home and educational training, attending to children's health needs, proper discipline, provision of material needs, involving children in chores, monitoring and supervision of children, setting of rules, regulations and principles to mention just a few.

Family management cannot be implemented in isolation from prudent use of money and appropriate allocation of time. Therefore, there is need for parents to set aside money and time for the running of home affairs. The use of money and time vary from one family to another, depending on the prevailing situation in a family.

FAMILY INCOME MANAGEMENT

Every family depends on its income for the provision of

family needs. So, it is very important to make the best use of it, by careful budgeting and management. Lack of good planning leads to indiscriminate spending that will eventually cause embarrassment and unhappiness to the family. For this reason, the adult family members should show maturity and understanding concerning their demands on parents' income so that everybody gets his or her fair share, without too much strain on the budget.

With such an understanding, there should be tolerance and compromise over the family plan of expenditure, for everyone's comfort. The sources of family income vary with different families according to their occupation. Some parents depend on wages or salaries, some are self-employed and some parents are retirees and therefore, depend on personal investments and pension allowances. Good money management should provide for a moderately comfortable living experience for all family members and this requires good knowledge about money management.

Families can achieve great success in money management with good planning, good monetary discipline, prioritization and proper allocation of money for family needs. Parents can categorize expenses into primary and secondary needs. Primary family needs include expenses on food, health, clothing and housing. These are basic or compulsory family expenses that cannot be avoided. Although, the father is the breadwinner in most homes, the wife should complement her husband's efforts and spend wisely. If the wife is the provider at home, the husband should show understanding and cooperate with her. Secondary needs cover expenses on children education, bills, transports, picnic, investments, savings, holidays, pocket money, family projects and so on and so forth.

Parents should train their children how to manage money because of the benefits that can be derived from it. Apart from the prudent use of money at home, children who are employed should be taught to invest their money in profit-yielding private and public firms or in government monetary instruments, shares, stocks, bonds, bills, treasury certificates, fixed deposits and other financial products. These are some of the investment opportunities parents should encourage their children to take part. Where there is surplus, parents can invest for the small children that are not yet working.

Proper money management, particularly in relation to investment will serve as additional source of income. No matter how small, families should invest part of their income. This advice is very important because the proceed of these investments in form of profits and dividends will also serve as reliable financial support during the ageing period to meet old age health problems and other urgent matters especially when the children are not around.

TIME MANAGEMENT AND SAFETY PRECAUTION

The modern housewife often plays a dual role in the changing patterns of family living. As a housewife, there are household duties to be performed, and as a salary earner, she goes out to work on strict schedules. All these activities are time consuming. It is therefore, very important that she develops the ability to manage time effectively to balance both. Efficient management of time can help minimize expenses on labor and the time spent in running a home, in other words, it means spending less time for a greater output of work.

The need for time management is the responsibility of both parents. Parents should train their children on the importance and benefits of time management. Parents should avoid unnecessarily strict adherence to time management at the expense of quality and satisfactory work. Parents need to use discretion in managing time.

To manage time effectively and efficiently, parents should plan and organize activities at home. These can be done in many ways. To succeed in implementing the plan and organization of activities, parents should prepare a roster for house chores and other activities such as recreation, academic, picnic, family discussions and so on. Parents should budget moderately flexible time for different activities, spread house chores for all the children, make necessary preparations in advance, use appropriate equipment if available, wash utensils immediately after use, disallow pillage of work, put utensil and every items in their proper places and so on. It is also necessary for parents to monitor and supervise work among children to make them versatile. The children will benefit very well from this method not only at home but wherever they find themselves.

It is wise time management to stick to safety and security precautions always. For example, unexpired fire extinguisher should be installed at strategic locations in the house, emergency telephone numbers of safety and security agencies must be within the reach of family members, reminder leaflets can be pasted on entry and exit doors for the family to check and switch off all electrical appliances immediately; after use, after power cut and before leaving the house. First-aid box containing medicine, bandage, plaster, scissors, etc must be available at home but placed out of reach of small children. When these safety and security precautions are observed at home, time will not only be saved. Life and property will also be saved and protected respectively.

Also, when parents implement sound planning and management in their day-to-day activities, it will bring family members closer together. It will save life and protect property. Parents will accomplish office work schedules with less stress and attend to family matters. Everyone will be more organized and less stressed. Families will make the best use of precious time, finances and other resources. It provides a way of passing family values. Children will develop the spirit of good planning and management. Many activities can be performed and completed. It will help children develop important skills. Family will find more time to have fun together.

CHAPTER 5

SECRET OF MARRIAGE HAPPINESS

Marriage is a lifetime contract. Married couples have many different roles to play. It is an unselfish concern for couples to do what is right for each other. What are some of the good behaviors expected of husbands and wives to keep them happy despite all odds?

Married couples should continue to forgive each other freely. The importance of **forgiveness** cannot be overemphasized in human relationship. This is even very vital among married couples because they are from different background. Moreover, imperfection which is a natural part of every person makes mistakes unavoidable. Mistakes can be corrected when there is understanding and readiness by either of the couple to admit to his or her error. With this perspective forgiveness will then become very handy in solving the problem. However, this negative trait, imperfection should not be used as a tool for willful provocation between each other.

The husband must be a **good provider**. It is the husband's responsibility to provide the material needs for his family. It is not an act of stupidity for the husband to work out with his wife a budget that will be agreeable to both of them. This creates room for understanding, particularly when there is a shortfall in domestic expenses.

There must be **mutual respect** and this cannot be gained but earned by how either of them reacts to specific and general issues that may arise. Mutual respect will result in happy and successful marriage if couples are considerate and honor each other.

Furthermore, the husband will be respected if he is steady, firm when and where necessary, strong, unselfish and balanced in decision making. Happiness can also be enhanced when the wife is in subjection to her husband. In turn, the husband should not be harsh and dictatorial in using his headship. Modest and humble lifestyles are better than pride and stubbornness and should be displayed by couples. These are fine qualities. Neither of the couples should see these qualities as weaknesses.

Everybody loves a **cheerful giver**. There is more happiness in giving than in receiving. The act of giving gift occasionally (not necessarily expensive gifts) will be greatly appreciated by each other. Apart from gifts, both of them need to give each other time, attention, thoughts and freely make expressions of endearment to each other.

Of paramount importance is **neatness** and **good hygiene.** These should always take priority position in the wife's duties. This will make the home a pleasant place to live. The husband needs to show recognition for his wife's physical and emotional make-up and also assign honor to her as a weaker but precious vessel. In addition, he should be kind, gentle and let her know that he cares instead of being forcefully overworked her. In this manner, he will gain his wife's support and loyalty.

Communication is the activity or process of expressing ideas and feelings or process of giving people information. In other words, communication can be achieved by talking, gesticulating, using signs or symbols, writing and even keeping silence. Regular communication (particularly by talking) enable married couples know and understand each other very well.

But where there is no communication or there is prolonged communication gap, many problems may develop. The cumulative adverse effect of this laxity could be separation or divorce. A loving husband will always converse with his wife about her activities, views, problems and so on. He will also encourage her in her projects and commend her for what she accomplished. All these proactive actions of the husband will move a wife to perform beyond expectation. The husband should avoid speaking alone, ending or dominating discussion always. He must listen to his wife's views and encourage her to express her thoughts and feelings freely. The lines of communication should always be opened in a warm and tension-free atmosphere.

Furthermore, the tone of voice and the choice of words are every important among couples. Good communication flourishes when there are gentle spoken words, gracious looks and gestures, kindness, understanding and tenderness. Continuous decent and polite communication among couples can be a source of comfort, can prevent anger and can provide relief to each other in terms of stress or disappointment. It is not possible to measure up perfectly but regular conversation will prevent or heal the wound of mistakes easily and lovingly.

SECTION 2

MARITAL PERIOD

CHAPTER 6

PREPARING AND CARING FOR BABY

The family is made up of a husband, a wife and children. The basic purpose of marriage is procreation. A marriage that is not blessed with children is obviously incomplete. Many reasons can be attributed to childlessness in married couples. This may include problems such as genetic, blood related, physiological abnormalities, disease, infection, etc. It is an inestimable blessing to have children, it is a source of joy and it strengthens marriage bond.

Couples have a right to have children. Their children have a corresponding right to have parents that will love and care for them. When a baby is born into a family, the parents experience emotions that are found in no other human relationship. Just holding their little one, watching it sleep, or seeing its wide smile brings them profound happiness and satisfaction.

Loving parents cherish their children. They train them to behave properly, polite and respectful. As the children develop in response to these efforts, parents feel proud and begin nurturing great hopes regarding them. Planning and preparing for children is an exciting, resource consuming, vital joint project among couples.

When preparing for child rearing, husband and wife need to discuss extensively on many important direct and indirect crucial matters, such as the time to have children, number of children, adjustment in schedules, readiness and ability of parents to provide for the physical, spiritual emotional needs of every child, provision of proper training and so on. Apart from the preparation mentioned above, it is very important for the wife to make some necessary personal preparation which include; preparation for parenthood, care for the pregnancy, preparation for delivery and so forth.

When a woman gets married, she looks forward to the time when she will have a baby. The period of pregnancy can be a great challenge. Some women go through it with excitement and anxiety whilst others go through it with great strain. During this period, it is important for the expectant mother to take care of herself and unborn baby. Among other things, a newly married woman should have an idea about the signs of pregnancy. She should also know the medical facilities which are available in her neighborhood and their locations, such as government approved maternity hospitals and clinics.

SIGNS OF PREGNANCY

When a woman is pregnant, she misses are menstrual period. Nausea and vomiting are early signs of pregnancy. Also, during the first few months, a pregnant woman may feel sick in the morning when she gets up. Other indicators include enlarged breast, frequent urination, dizziness and so forth.

CARING FOR PREGNANCY

Caring for the pregnant mother before and after birth is a combined responsibility of the married couples. But a deep sense of understanding, consideration, help, support and assistance is needed from the husband because this will have a direct effect in preserving and protecting both the life of the fetus (unborn baby) and the expectant mother.

On the part of the mother, she must register with government approved maternity hospital for regular ante-natal and post-natal check up, she must follow medical counsels strictly on matters such as the type of food, types of beverages and drugs that must be taken, type of exercise and work that must be done and the ones to abstain from. Also important is proper hygiene, avoidance of mosquito infested areas, avoidance of risky activities and risk-prone environment and so forth.

REASONS FOR ANTE-NATAL AND POST-NATAL CHECK UP

Ante-natal check up refers to the regular medical consultations made by a pregnant woman before birth. Some of the reasons for these compulsory consultations are to enable medical doctor examine her, to examine the fetus position and heartbeat, to effect necessary treatment, to monitor development, changes and proffer appropriate medical counsel.

Post-natal check up refer to the regular after birth visits

made by a nursing mother with her baby to the maternity hospital where she delivered the baby. Some of the reasons for this visit include; the examination of both the nursing mother and the baby, examination of the baby's weight, immunization, vaccination, demonstration lessons for the mother on suitable baby foods and so forth.

PREPARATION FOR DELIVERY

It is most important for the expectant mother to deliver her baby at the maternity hospital where she registered for consultation. Prior to this, she must get the materials and the utensils required ready. These include clothing materials, bedding materials, toiletries, feeding equipment, sterilizers, containers, cotton wool and other necessary materials required by the hospital.

BENEFITS OF INTENSIVE BREAST FEEDING

Motherly care and attention cannot be overstressed on issues concerning babies. For example, regular breast feeding for between one to two years protect babies against infections. Breast milk is easily digested, helps in emptying the bowels, enhances physiology of the baby, it contains balanced nutrients, it has the right temperature, it does not require preparation, it is clean, it helps babies exercise their jaws. The mother also benefits in terms of reduced risk of breast cancer, stimulation of internal healing and it is economical. Security and love is rapidly strengthened due to mother-baby relationship while breast feeding the baby.

Children are rewards and bundles joy for parents.

Children can be males alone, females alone or combination of both sexes. Parents (particularly the father), should accept anyone of these two sexes. It is needless to attach importance to a particular sex. This is because the father is the determinant of a baby's sex. It is advisable for the couple to allow proper child spacing. The method adopted vary from one couple to another and this depends on prevailing circumstances, mutual agreement, health reasons and many other factors.

There are situations where a couple deicide not start having children immediately after marriage. In his case, it is advisable to consult medical personnel for necessary safe or preventive measures. The advice is vitally important because it will prevent unwanted pregnancy and abortion. More importantly, it will safeguard the life of the mother.

CHAPTER 7

COMBINED ROLES OF THE FAMILY

Parental role in rearing children is exciting but it presents a challenge, and for the best results, the challenge needs to be met by both parents. Both parents are responsible for a child's development and birth. In a similar manner, both of them should intensify unity, humility and sincerity in raising the children.

Parents should understand and be able to harmonize their roles to enable them meet the needs of their children. It is desirable for the father to exercise his headship, but if he goes to the extreme, the outcome may be regrettable. It is equally compulsory for the mother to share in training the children but to take over this duty to the exclusion of the father will weaken the family structure.

The father and the mother should co-operate in training the children. If parents properly considered the wishes and preferences of each other before taking decisions, the children will imitate this co-operative example and be able to take reasonable decisions always. In addition to this, there should be enough parental supervision to see that sound principles are followed, that the children's safety is not endangered and that the rights of others are not infringed upon.

The general or combined roles of parents are many and vary from one parent to another but the underlying required universal principle for parents is to act in unison for the positive development of the children.

In homes where the children are grown up, home activities can be carried out by the parents and the grown up children together. Some of the attitudes required by parents and children for this suggestion to work include; living within family's income, creating and spending time together, developing spirit of helpfulness and so on.

LIVE WITHIN YOUR INCOME

If every member of the family co-operate by living within the family income, it will spare the family many problems. Parents should agree to keep life simple. Also, children should learn contentment, not demanding things that the family budget cannot support. For example, the temptation to buy things you cannot afford, getting into debt, has led many families into shipwreck. Also, budget can be prepared for home expenses which will focus on needs and not wants. This will prevent wasteful expenses that can harm the family's economic situation.

Some of the areas in which families can combine activity include pooling funds for picnic, buying of equipment for the home, donation to organizations, contribution for the less privileged, project execution and so on.

Children should not be forced to get involved in these activities. Instead, they should be encouraged. This attitude places a greater sense of worth, belonging and responsibility on the children. The children will also learn generosity and always show concerned feelings for fellow human beings.

CREATE AND SPEND TIME TOGETHER

This is one of the best ways a family can stay united. All members should willingly pool their spare time. For example, children may have to sacrifice some favorite programs, sporting events, outing with friends and other personal activities. Also, parents can sacrifice their leisure time used for personal interests and personal activities for combined family activities. Given this provision parents can plan activities with the family, perhaps how to spend weekends or vacations together plan something that every family member will look forward to and enjoy. This type of arrangement is vitally important because the whole family (particularly the children) will enjoy quality and quantity time that will further strengthen family bond and happiness.

DEVELOP SPIRIT OF HELPFULNESS

Spirit of helpfulness is not coercive, it is voluntary. Spirit of helpfulness should not be an eye-service, it must be genuine. This spirit is very useful in that it is motivated by the willingness to improve a particular situation and to share with others in many different ways.

Another form of contribution to a happy family spirit is combined effort in housekeeping. The parents should make an arrangement whereby every member of the family can share in home activities such as cleaning and maintenance, working in the garden, laundry work, cooking and so forth.

Each family member, including the younger ones could be assigned some part of a task. Instead of being idle and loitering around when the house is untidy and dirty, children can perform many essential roles in the house. This spirit of helpfulness and co-operation will result in genuine friendship and companionship, which build family unity.

It is important to state clearly that the involvement of children in home activity which requires money is voluntary and should not be misunderstood by children as failure, inability, unwillingness or weakness of parents to accomplish their roles. Instead, it is part of good home training and management which teaches children reasonable use of initiative, good sense of responsibility and development of helpful and co-operative spirit. Remember, there is more happiness in giving than there is in receiving. Apart from the combined roles of the families discussed, there are specific roles for the mother and the father. What are some of these specific roles?

SOME SPECIFIC ROLES OF THE WIFE

Individual member of the family has specific roles to play. The position of the wife is always secondary to that of the husband. This is a divine placement for the wife. However, the wife's position in the household is one of recognized importance and it must be appreciated by the family members. The wife or the mother has natural responsibilities that cannot be performed by the husband or the father. Commonest among these are breast-feeding of the baby, understanding, guiding and training the growing girl child on some puberty and physiological changes to mention just a few.

There is always a special closeness between the mother and the child during the pre-weaning and the early years after weaning. A new born baby is totally dependent on its mother for its immediate needs. If she lovingly supplies the needs, the baby feels secure. The baby must be well fed, kept clean and warm. The baby can be very active and understand loving relationship if the mother cultivate the habit of smiling, stroking, cuddling, touching, talking, kissing and playing with the baby. Other family members can do all these too, but the mother's pleasant aroma can easily be perceived. In the case of a girl child, the mother has crucial roles in monitoring, preparing and training on matters such as: menstruation; how it looks, the signs, how it can be catered for and other related effects.

Scientific studies show that the child can start learning immediately after birth and that the first few years are the most important. During those years, the mother's love is crucial. If she succeeds in showing and teaching love, she can do lasting good; if she fails, this will cause serious harm. Being a good mother is one of the most challenging and rewarding jobs a woman can do. Therefore, the mother should devote enough time for the baby instead of keeping the baby in a child care center permanently or for an unnecessary long period of time. However, the use of decent child care centers is not ruled out but parents should not depend on these centers for the upbringing of their children.

Furthermore, instead of spending every leisure time in attending parties and other social ceremonies that are not compulsory and not necessary, it will be highly beneficial if the wife or mother can be at home and be a guide and friend to the children, it will certainly contribute greatly toward building strong bonds that will help keep the family together through thick and thin. A woman can contribute outstandingly to make a home happy, secure and functional.

SOME SPECIFIC ROLES OF THE HUSBAND

In today's world, there are many obstacles a family head may face in order to provide for his household. Economic hardships are common globally, as are high rate of unemployment, rising cost of living, layoffs, poor salary package, employer's exploitation and a host of other problems. The husband usually makes the living and when he comes back home from work he may be tired, and still may have another income-generating jobs and home duties to perform. A responsible husband does well to remember that he is performing a divine assignment. Because of this, he will always make necessary and timely provisions for his family members.

Besides provision of food, clothing, shelter and healthcare, the husband should make time for his wife and his children. He communicate with his family, set time aside for discussions on family projects, leisure activities, general and other specific family matters. With this type of organization; family life, unity, confidence, loyalty and happiness are built up.

It is the primary role of the husband to make firm and flexible rules, regulations and instructions. The type of rules made and adopted will depend on the family, situation, purpose and objectives to be achieved. Also of great importance is the type of punishment or discipline to be meted for erring children. In view of this, the children will understand that to belong to the family; certain conducts are acceptable and that certain actions and attitudes are not allowed. The children will also have a clear knowledge of what the family stands for and the type of examples the parents show. Children want to feel the security of belonging, so let them feel your approval and acceptance when they meet the home standards.

Finally, the role of both parents is to provide a home atmosphere of love. If this is felt by the children, they will feel free to disclose their problems and mistakes. The fact that the children know they can communicate and be understood and that matters will be handled with loving concern, the home will not just be a shelter but also a place that is safe and peaceful. Children are very observant. They sense the attitudes and observe the things practiced around them. Therefore, they sense the parents' feelings whether these are hostile or relaxed peacefulness.

People are judged by their actions more than by their words. Children, too, may not give as much attention to words as to actions of their parents. Their parents should back up their words with appropriate actions. While executing this challenging work of parenthood, both parents can accomplish it with happy results by avoiding extreme freedom and by avoiding unnecessary rigidity. In other words, a balance should be maintained. Do children have any responsibility in the family?

CHAPTER 8

RESPONSIBILITIES OF CHILDREN

Our parents gave each of us something we cannot give to them in return. For whatever else we may owe them, we owe them our present life. Without them, we would not be. For this one most important reason, children should honor their parents greatly. In view of this, children should feel a deep sense of indebtedness to their parents. Children can contribute to parents' joy and satisfaction by showing genuine respect for their position, listening to their counsel and being obedient.

Children should be ready to acquire wisdom, knowledge, and tap from the good experience of their parents, if they want to be responsible in the society. In other words, the parents are older and are more experienced and as a result, they are wiser in coping with problem of life. Children will readily accept this, if they do not see their parents as old-fashioned people with unworkable ideas. This advice is timely, appropriate and very necessary because it is not unusual for some youth to think themselves wiser than their parents. And therefore, should not feel the advice of their parents is outdated just because they are no longer youths. It is only the parents not the young, inexperienced shallow minded friends or companions can provide wise and practical counsels.

Hardworking, initiative and creative children are parents' pride. Parents are at ease both at home and away from home when children are not lazy and are able to use their discretion properly. These types of children will always perform above parents' expectation. That is, these children will do more without being asked, thereby bringing satisfaction to their parents. These valuable qualities will even attract positive assessment from the public and in turn bring honor to the entire family.

To further boost the performance of children and fully prepare them for future challenges, parents should teach their children all domestic work without separating specific work for a particular child. For example, male and female children should be taught how to prepare nutritious meals, soup, snacks, how to do repair work, how to bath and dress for baby and so forth. This may sound amusing but it is very important that parents include this method in child training.

Furthermore, parents should not overlook uncertainties and unforeseen circumstances. When these happen, the child may not have any alternative but to face the challenges immediately regardless of the type of task and whether it is interesting or not. The responsibility of children here is to learn how to handle different types of domestic work as this makes life's challenges a fun instead of a burden.

Children (particularly the young ones) generally have the wrong feelings that discipline is wickedness, acts of hatred, denial of freedom, denial of enjoyment and denial of personal rights when applied by parents. Discipline is one of the pivotal trainings that parents owe their children and it is one of the responsibilities that children must accept with appreciation. It is better to have parents who instill discipline than to have ones who do not care. Appropriate and timely discipline will not allow the development of many bad habits in children.

Hostility, disrespect, unreasonable envy, use of dirty languages, selfishness, carefree attitude, fight, bitter complains and a host of other bad habits among the children make the home a hostile place instead of a haven. Children have the responsibility to avoid these behaviors completely. Parent, therefore, should make earnest effort in inculcating the right discipline.

Grown up children should show deep appreciation and care for their parents in all aspects of life. Just as children need parental love, parents equally need love and reassuring attention from their children particularly when they are old. Therefore, children should not turn away or abandon their parents in times of need. From youth on into adulthood, children have many vital roles to play in the life of their parents.

Many children are a source of grief, regret, failure, shame and disappointment. All these bad consequences can be avoided when parents play their roles at home properly and children respond positively to discipline.

EFFECTIVE DISCIPLINE WITH CARE

Obedient, loving, well-mannered children do not just

happen. They are molded and produced through good examples and reasonable cautious discipline. The rising cases of crimes and juvenile delinquency is not limited to a few nations, it is a global plague and can be attributed to either willful disobedience by children or lack of regular and proper training and discipline. In the special context of family management, what is discipline?

Discipline is the practice of training children to obey rules and orders and correcting or punishing them if they disobey. It is a form of controlled behavior or situation. It is a method of training a child's mind, body or behavior. Also, discipline is training that corrects the mind and heart of children. Discipline is aimed at giving children instructions that correct wrong view points, mold their mental faculties and course of conduct. Discipline is an essential part of parental love, care and protection designed to promote their lasting welfare. Acceptance of discipline makes a child wise, able to use knowledge aright, and thus helps a child to avoid much pains and suffering in his or her lifetime.

The erroneous understanding of some parents is that discipline involves merely speaking to children in threatening voices or scolding them. Different children require different kinds of disciplinary measures. Some children are not corrected by mere words. For these types of children, occasional punishment administered for disobedience may be lifesaving.

When punishment is administered, a child should be

made to understand why he or she is being disciplined in that manner. This type of discipline should have a limit and commensurate with a child's age. Parents should not hastily apply punishment when they are offended or when a wrongdoing has been committed. This is necessary to prevent permanent wound or injury on the child. Parents should never leave a child rejected after discipline. However, appropriate disciplinary action should not be compromised when this is the best method to use. Parents should not be too lax, too severe, or inconsistent. A balance should always be maintained.

Sometimes a child's offence may not be intentional. In this case, parents should use sound judgement, proper assessment and discernment for the erring child, as well as the situation and the offence committed before administering discipline.

Parents should put reasonable guidelines, standards, rules and regulations in place to enable them apply the right disciplinary action(s) as the case may be within specified limits. This will enable children experience some measure of freedom, feel at ease, see themselves as members of the family and manifest deep sense of concern, responsibility and reasonableness because they have limits that they must conform to its requirements. This in turn, will disallow children from floundering on their own and avoid possible fatal consequences.

Guidelines and limitations should be clear with provisions for warnings and forgiveness. Parents should not expect too much or too little particularly from the young ones. The level or intensity of discipline should be commensurate to a child's age. Once reasonable rules have been established and children understand them, parents can then enforce them properly and consistently. It takes determination on the part of parents to show firmness when a child tends to disobey their order. Parents must be flexible, be firm when necessary and be relaxed as situation permits. This will enable children develop a kind of check and control within themselves and will not become bold in bad habits. Discipline should be based on sound reasoning and justice.

Communication should not be isolated from discipline. That is, parents should let the child know why he or she is being disciplined. In this manner the child will not a wrong perception of discipline as wickedness or hatred. Discipline and communication is even very vital and necessary during the early years of a child. This is because a child's willingness or unwillingness to respond to adult demands, rules or control will begin to manifest. Likewise, the need for obedience and respect when necessary for authority, seniors or elders should be inculcated progressively. It is logical to agree that children will understand obedience as something they have to express not because their parents or the authority are bigger or stronger but because it is required.

Moreover, when a child has been made aware of his or her mistake and understands why discipline was administered, parents should avoid talking about the child's mistake or offence repeatedly. This will not speed up correction, instead it will aggravate problem. The child may consider this as rejection by the parents and/or isolation from other children in the family.

Finally, effective discipline can be given in different ways. Just as different children will require different treatment, the natural ways a child behaves or reacts to situation or people and the natural qualities of a child must be considered. For example, one child may require punishment while another may require rebuke.

Furthermore, discipline can be employed to make a child feel the unpleasant consequences of wrong behavior. That is, parents should let the child correct his or her offence and apologize with a sincere promise. Another form of discipline is the denial of privileges for a time in other to drive home the needed lesson. Whatever the method used, children need to be shown that they must bear the outcome of their behavior. This teaches them responsibility. Parents on their part should apply discipline on the basis of fairness and justice.

CHAPTER 9

TEACH CHILDREN GOOD HOME TRAINING

Training is the process of learning the skills that you need to do a job. In the special context of the family, home training can be defined as the process of teaching or inculcating good morals or good behaviors that children need to live a decent and responsible life. The former definition can be described as external, educational or vocational training while the latter can be described as internal, domestic or home training.

The two types of trainings are compulsory for every child to be successful, responsible and survive in life. In conformity with the words of wisdom, charity begins at home. The need for a balanced training must be stressed so as to remind and/or guide parents on the significance of this primary and lifelong parental responsibility. What contrasting views do parents have about this subject? When should this training start? How should this training be carried out? Is love relevant in training? Should parent compare children?

Some parents permissively leave their children without making any primary training efforts. Some leave their children to their own devices, thinking that children should be raised in a spirit of freedom. Or because they are so busy, some parents may not create time to give their children careful attention and needed training. Still, some parents feel that their children's schooling is the only vital thing, so they give their children almost unlimited freedom as long as they get excellent grades in school and get into prestigious institutions. As a contrary opinion to the views above, some parents considered it a must to ensure that all necessary trainings are made available to children. The opinion of the last school of thought is based on the fact that untrained children constitute the greatest number of crimes of every kind, violence, hooliganism and rape to mention just a few.

Home training should start from infancy and continue for as long as the children remain with the parents. But there will be variation in the intensity, sequence, regularity, time, type and the method of training or teaching to be inculcated in the children. These must correspond to the growth and changes in the children.

A baby's brain at birth is only one fourth the weights it will be in adulthood. But the brain grows so rapidly that in just two years, it reaches three fourth of its adult weight. Besides, a child's intelligence grows as much during the first four years of life as during the next thirteen. In view of these, parents need to recognize the infants' yearnings to learn and this should start right away. From this time onward, the little ones are busy taking in information, filing it away, adding to it and drawing conclusions and so on.

Love through care and affection is the first lesson to be taught. Though infants cannot respond to talk and they cannot communicate at their age; they should be talked to in a grown up decent speech using correct words and pronunciations. Gesticulation and/or demonstration can be combined with oral communication for a better and faster understanding and learning.

The parents should be able to read loud for the infant to hear and be prepared to answer numerous questions from those ones that can talk. The answers should be very brief, direct and simple. Pictures, objects, natural things such as; flowers, animals, rivers, body parts can be used efficiently and effectively in responding to the child's questions. Remember that your baby is learning from not just by what you say but also by how you say it and by the tone of voice used in responding. Therefore, parents' responses, motives emotions, feelings and behavior should be proper and fit the situation always.

Every child is different with a unique personality. This trait should be helped to develop in harmony with a child's inherited potentials and gifts. If parents trained each child to develop its inherited strengths and abilities, the child will not need to feel envy at the success or accomplishments of other children. Every child should be loved and appreciated for what he or she is. While helping the child to control or overcome wrong inclinations, they should not try to force the child into a predetermined mold. Instead, they should guide the child to the best use of its own good personality traits. Therefore, parents should avoid comparing one child unfavorably with another. The child may take this as rejection. The child may feel hurt, downhearted and may likely become hostile if this treatment continues. On the other hand, the child presented as superior may become haughty and incur the dislike of others.

As a parent, your love and acceptance should never be dependent upon how one child compares with another. Comparison is not completely ruled out because it helps a lot in checking, controlling and enhancing good performance. Balance and limits should be put in mind. Always find positive things in your child and praise the child sincerely. If there is need for instructions or corrections, this should be done reasonably. School work and other school activities should not be in the hands of teachers alone. Parents should check all these regularly and liaise with the teachers while also paying impromptu visits to the child in the school.

The issues concerning parental training cannot be exhausted because of the different kinds of factors or situation that affect parents and children. This primarily has to do with parents' upbringing and discipline background. This will have a lasting effect on children. In other words, it will show if parents maintained, reduced, improved, completely searched and developed new training and values in raising their children. Or whether the parents abandoned training and discipline and live everything at the children's discretion.

The simple unavoidable requirement is for the parents to perform their primary responsibility of training their children (from infancy) always. This is a solid foundation that will mold children's behavior throughout their lifetime. Finally, it is possible for parents to raise decent and responsible children by devoting sufficient time to teach their children good home training. But good home training is not the only training children require. In addition to good home training, children need good quality education or skills to take care of themselves and their family in the future. What type of education and skills acquisition are available for children? Why is vocational skills acquisition a decent alternative for children? Where can children acquire skills? And what can children benefit by acquiring vocational skills?

CHAPTER 10

THE NEED FOR QUALITATIVE EDUCATION OR SKILLS

Education is a process of teaching, training and learning, especially in schools (primary, secondary and tertiary institutions), to improve knowledge and develop skills. Education is a process of imparting or acquiring knowledge and skills. Education can be accomplished through the process of explanation and repetition, personal observation, experimentation, research and so on. What is qualitative education? Qualitative education is the acquisition of balanced and sustainable knowledge and skills useful for immediate and future application not just as a qualified job seeker but also as a certified job creator. It is important to state clearly that education must start from home.

Some parents have no time while some abandoned children education to the school teacher alone. These parents fail to realize that they have to prepare their children during the pre-school years to build a solid foundation for their children. This is called basic home education. This education covers the provision of necessary basic educational instructions for the children. This basic education must be consistent, it must be taught in a relax condition and within an absorption time frame that is commensurate with age. The target for this home programme is the pre-school small children.

Parents must develop a coherent pre-school educational programme so as to create awareness, to develop mental faculty, to make advance preparation, to enhance understanding, to assess a child's intelligence and so on. Interest is an important factor in education. Also, parents must make it a habit to be interested in their children and observe what goes on around them.

In the early stages of training, parents can train their children to be good listeners. Children vary in disposition and attention span. Parents need discernment to be able to assess their children and help them learn to listen attentively. At home, parents should arrange convenient time for their young children to sit quietly and read or look at the pictures in simple educational books and publications.

The objective of this teaching is for the children to acquire necessary basic educational knowledge and benefit from a moderately or reasonably organized teaching programme at home. To achieve this vital objective, it is compulsory for parents to carefully observe and keep in mind the following points: ability of every child to pay attention, knowledge retention capacity of every child, personal reading habit, willingness to study, inquisitiveness, ability to answer questions properly and correctly, subject(s) of interest (e.g. science, artwork, technical work,) and so on. Children will be most attentive when the teaching environment is congenial with programme conveniently and timely structured. Repetition is the mother of knowledge. It is true that imparting knowledge in young children or kids takes time and it is difficult. This therefore, requires parents to assess a child's performance regularly by integrating short revision periods at intervals of teaching programme.

FORMAL EDUCATION

This is the type of education which follows an agreed or official method of knowledge and skill acquisition in a primary school, college, technical institute or university. Formal education involves registration, attending lesson and lecture classes in school or on the internet, taking part in science practical, projects, fieldworks, researches, tests, examinations, acceptance of results, certificates or degrees and so forth. In other words, formal education is an organized or procedural method of acquiring knowledge or skill. Formal education comprises of three different levels or stages namely; primary, secondary and tertiary levels.

Primary education is the first formal education for school age children usually between age three and ten. The age of a child at entry and the type of school chosen by parents depends on income, point of entry (nursery or primary), literacy level of parents and so on. Primary education is made up of nursery and direct primary classes. Regardless of the school choice made by parents, it is not advisable for parents to send a child to a long distance or boarding school at the primary education level. If parents heed this advice, they will be able to monitor their children and assess their performance. Parents will be able to offer the needed assistance promptly. Also, parent-child intimacy will be stronger and the child will not be molded or re-molded by any external persons, factors or influences. At the completion of primary education, a child is expected to know the rudimentary of education. These include; how to read, how to write, simple hygiene, how to solve simple arithmetic, spellings, pronunciations, short memory exercises and other vital learning and elementary educational knowledge.

Secondary school is the second stage or second level of formal education. At this level, a child is expected to apply and build on the elementary knowledge acquired in primary school. In secondary schools, every subject is treated to a reasonable and commensurate limit based on specified syllabus. And children are allowed to specialize in different subject combination categories namely; science, commercial, literal arts, pure arts and so on. Academic performance and interest are some of the key determinants of students' choice of subject combination. Parents can only be helpful as additional (optional) guidance in addition to the school's educational counselors and not the career decision maker for children. In other words, parents must not enforce a profession or career on their children. Subject specializations in secondary schools prepare children for future professional courses or career in tertiary institutions.

Tertiary education is the final stage or final level of formal education. Some examples of tertiary educational establishments include but not limited to colleges of education, specialized institutes, mono-techniques, poly-techniques, universities and so on. Most academic programmes in tertiary institutions are job-market focused. In other words, the training and skills acquired are the necessary theoretical and practical skills for individual's choice of profession. At the completion of tertiary education, students graduate with different qualifications and become specialist or professionals such as engineers, doctors, agriculturists, teachers, administrators, research scientist, pharmacists, builders, lawyers, food technologist and so on.

It is advisable for students in tertiary institutions to pursue professions which have high market demand and contribute to economic development and also be prepared not just as job seekers but also as job creators. This aspect of family management is very vital. The aim is to remind or inform parents about the need to be deeply involved in the academic pursuit of their children. Education is the greatest and the most durable asset parents must provide for their children.

VOCATIONAL OR ENTERPRENEURAL SKILLS

Children have different talents and abilities. Some are exceptionally bright, some are averagely brilliant and some are below average in academic performance. It is obvious from these simple analyses that not all children can acquire tertiary education and qualifications. Apart from the reasons just mentioned, some children are constrained by parents' little or lack of formal educational trainings and/or poverty. When children do not have the opportunity of acquiring tertiary education, the hope is not lost. The alternative to this is to enroll for vocational or entrepreneurial training. It is necessary to point out that acquisition of vocational or entrepreneurial skills are not restricted to these set of people alone. Those who have tertiary education can equally register for this special training or skills for many good reasons.

Vocational centers are organized skill acquisition specialized schools established purposely to provide the necessary job and small business skills required to develop an individual to be self-employed and job-creating. The cost of enrolling in these schools is much cheaper than in tertiary institutions. Most of the trainings are short-termed. Training period and training method also depend on educational background, interest and ability of trainees, type of vocation, health condition of trainee and so on. The training period covers between few months to about four years. Certificates are issued to trainees at the end of the programmes.

It is advisable for prospective students to have a minimum of secondary education before registering for training. Some of the advantages of these educational backgrounds include; ability to comprehend easily, creativity, ability to manage resources efficiently, high job opportunities and so on. Those who decide to acquire this training should not be seen as failure or irrelevant in the society. As a matter of fact, this category of people account for the greater part of employment for job seekers in many countries. In addition to this, they are the backbone for economic development in the society.

Production, packaging, marketing, supply, distribution,

waste recycling and other value added processes are integrated in the training and skill acquisition programmes where necessary. This will enable trainees produce and take their products to the final consumers with little stress. Vocational or entrepreneurial skills are acquired in many government and private skill acquisition centers, directorate of training and job creation centers, local and international, human development centers, human empowerment institutes, labor and capacity building establishments, small and medium enterprises development agencies and a host of other skill acquisition centers and agencies.

Acquisition of vocational training or skills enables trainees to be skillful in different jobs and varieties of small and medium enterprises. Some of these include; furniture making, auto-repair, plumbing works, stationery production, fashion designing, electrical repairs, tiles production, welding work, livestock keeping, wood and metal carving, snacks and beverage production, bead making, feed production, art work, crop production, interior decoration, candle production, hair-dressing, upholstery work, hat and cap production, toy production, bakery business, canteen services, pottery work, photography, painting, rental services, printing work, leather work, carpet production, business center services, and so forth.

Trainees for vocational skills need not worry about how to source funds or loan to finance their businesses. Funds and loan can be accessed in government and private financial organizations. Some of the financial organizations and agencies that provide financial backing for small and medium enterprises include but not limited to; government and private credit agencies, international business grant organization, micro-finance banks, and so on. Besides, some vocational centers and financial organizations provide equipment, materials and working capital or business establishment capital to be paid over a reasonable period of time with very small interest. Most of these financial sources requested for guarantors instead of collaterals that cannot be made available by the trainees.

Apart from the packaging and marketing skills integrated into the training programme, government also established different firms and agencies to add value and speed up product sale and transfer. These include; product packaging and marketing agencies, bulk purchasing agencies, export processing zones, product research centers, free trade zones, and a host of others.

Giving the vital roles of government, private and non-governmental agencies, acquisition of vocational or entrepreneurial skills should be seen as decent alternatives for children to succeed and to make a good living in life. Parents can encourage their children who have educational certificate only to try and acquire a skill or some skills that can be established and make them self employed so as to counter economic problems in future.

CHAPTER 11

SOUND MORAL PRINCIPLES AND VALUES

Moral values are the foundation that will shape a child's perception, behavioral disposition, assessment and proper appraisal of issues and situations. Achievement of excellent moral values for children is based on reasonable principles that will serve as guides or controls. Principles are moral rules or strong beliefs that influence actions. Principles can be defined as laws, rules, or theories that actions or reactions are based.

Sound moral values are integral part of parents' duties for their children. Although school teachers and bosses have important contributory roles to play, the major role is in the hands of parents. Values are beliefs about what is right or wrong, what is important, what is acceptably decent and what is reasonable in life.

Today many parents are confused as to what the true values of life are. As a result, many children are never given a set of values. Some parents even doubt their right to inculcate good morals in their children. If parents allowed this feeling to overwhelm their right to shape their children for the best, the outcome will be very bad for children.

Sometimes parents may be adversely affected too. The scene of the world is changing rapidly in many ways. Some of the noticeable changes include; social, cultural and moral changes to mention just a few. A child shows what he or she is by what he or she does. Most children are raised in ever changing morally degraded environment and this present a great challenge for parents. If parents do not provide the right moral values for their children at the appropriate time, some outside sources will provide it based on their objectives. Some of these external sources include; television, radio, magazines, friends, internet, journals and so on. Therefore, it is very important for parents to start teaching moral values to their children from young childhood.

Sound moral principles enable children to develop or cultivate their power of reasoning. For example, some grown up children will just do whatever they are told to do without thinking about the positive or negative outcomes. This is because they lack sound moral principles that will guide them to think or reason properly before making decisions or before taking actions.

Crucial issues of moral importance that require prompt and regular attention of parents include; proper use of drugs, proper view of sex, proper use of alcohol, decent dressing, decent hair styles, courtesy, need to be law-abiding, respect for authority, care and concern for lives and property, avoidance of obscene language, avoidance of violence, humility and a host of other moral issues. It is necessary to state that subject of morality goes beyond sex or sexual relationship alone as many people understand. Therefore, it is important to note that the exact opposite of the behaviors mentioned above are rampant among majority of youth and many adults globally.

To lay a solid foundation in inculcating sound moral values in children, parents are expected to set good examples in speech and in conduct when giving instructions or rules. Otherwise, the children will quickly assume that the parents are 'double tongued' and unserious. Therefore, parents' good examples are the first teacher and the best educator in teaching moral values.

Finally, parents should use every opportunity at their disposal to build in their children a set of values that can sustain them throughout their lives. Yes, helping children meet their needs take efforts. But the rewards are worth it. These set of true values will prepare the children against avoidable errors and wrongdoings, it will enhance the children's moral fiber and save the parents heartaches in their later years.

TEACH YOUR CHILDREN COURTESY

Gone are the days when courtesy was a sign of good moral training. In other words, lack of courtesy is rampant in words and actions of most children nowadays. What is courtesy? How can children show courtesy in their dealings with people?

Courtesy is a polite behavior that shows respect for other people. Courtesy is a polite way of talking or doing things always. Furthermore, courtesy means having or showing good manners and respect for the feelings of others.

Besides teaching children courtesy, parents must show

this essential quality in words and in actions. Humility, respect and proper use of initiative are some of the prerequisite virtues of courtesy. In addition, parents should teach their children to show courtesy always regardless of socio-cultural differences, geographical locations, tribal, nationality, status or age differences.

Some courtesy expressions that should be taught by parents include; please, kindly, could you, could you please, thank you, I am very grateful, I will appreciate….., I am sorry, please pardon me and so forth. It is an act of courtesy when young ones assist elders or seniors.

HUMILITY AND RESPECT

For a child to behave with courtesy, the child needs to show humility. In other words, the child must be humble. What is humility? How can a child be humble? Humility is the opposite of pride. A child is said to have humility if the child is not proud and does not believe that he or she is better than or superior to other people. If a child is humble, it does not mean that the child is from a poor family or the child is from a low social status. A humble child is not foolish. Instead, a humble child is wise. His or her display of humility is a reflection of good home training, acceptance of parental training and readiness to practice what he or she learn from his or her parents. A humble child or person is accommodating and hardly gets into trouble where people want to display pride.

Similarly, a child should respect people, laws, beliefs,

authorities, customs, rights, and so on reasonably.

CHAPTER 12

MANAGING GROWN-UP CHILDREN

The expectation and joy of every parent is to see their infant grow to an adult. During the period of growth and development, many visible and invisible changes such as physical, mental and emotional development will be noticeable and manifest in their behaviors. In parallel with these changes, parents need to fine tune how they treat and manage their children. This is very important because as children grow up, parental responsibility changes and increases. These changes may be gradual in some children and slightly rapid in others. Grown-up children can be described to include teenagers and adults.

As children grow to adulthood, they will eventually make very weighty decision for themselves. Parents should not always agree with all decisions taken by their children so as to protect them from the adverse outcomes of wrong decision. Also, grown-up children may want to be independent and may resent limits placed on them by their parents.

When children become adult, the period can be exciting and they can also be confusing. Children who realized the latter effect will understand that they still need skillful direction from their parents. And for the fact that they are facing more complex issues than before, they will be moved to recognize that their parents are well qualified as the best counselors because they are more experienced in life and have proved their loving concern over many years. Hence, at this stage in their life, wise children will not turn away from their parents.

Parents need to have a balanced view of child rearing. Some parents severely restrict and discipline their children while others are permissive, not providing the necessary guidelines that would protect their inexperienced children. It is not always easy to strike a balance between these two extremes. But a balance has to be maintained. Children require different treatment in terms of monitoring, supervision, etc. The bottom line is that parents should not confuse love with permissiveness thereby failing to set and enforce clear, consistent and reasonable rules.

Parents are happy to see their young children growing strong and healthy from childhood to adulthood. Similarly, they will feel happy when their adult children begin to move from complete dependence to appropriate self-reliance. But during this period, parents should not be surprised when they experience occasional stubbornness or uncooperative attitude from their children.

As difficult as it may be, parents need to avoid responding negatively to any reasonable requests from their children for greater freedom. This is not to say that all reasonable requests should be granted by parents. Parents need sound judgement in this type of situation. In a wholesome way, a child needs to grow as an individual. However, freedom brings with it accountability. Therefore, parents should allow their adult children to experience the consequences of some of their decisions and actions.

In a situation where a child wants to take a wrong step, parents should disallow this and stand by their decision no matter how smart or convincing the child may be. Why rejecting a child's request in a calm and polite manner, parents should always explain the reasons for saying no.

Children need the security of consistent discipline and rules. In other words, parents need not be changing rules or decision frequently; otherwise the children will assume they are not serious. If however, adult children receive help and encouragement needed in coping under different circumstances, they will grow up to be more stable. Well-thought-out boundaries give children room to grow while also protecting them from harm.

When parents strive for a balance between fair latitude and firm boundaries that are clearly marked, most children will feel less inclined to disobey. As a result of this, parents can be comforted to know that when peace, stability and love exist within the household, the children usually flourish.

Due to imperfection, mankind is not free from mistakes that sometimes could lead to serious problems. This is more so for the inexperienced children. When children make mistakes and get into serious problems, parents should not overreact. It is also very important to avoid uncontrolled wrath and bitterness. This is because the future of the children depend partly on how they are treated during their difficult times.

Consequently, children will feel free to discuss their problems. In solving the problem of a child that has done wrong, parents should let other members of the family learn from the mistakes of the one being corrected and how the repetition of the mistakes can be avoided in future.

COMMUNICATE REGULARLY WITH CHILDREN

The economic situation in many countries is not improving as people anticipated. This makes it mandatory for people to work overtime, combine different jobs or even work in two or more organizations to make ends meet. The trend is ever increasing and parents are the most affected. In families where both parents are salary earners, this economic depression has a serious negative effect particularly in setting time aside for household matters.

For example, the time that many parents spend with their children is reducing. While at home, parents have to do many housework and other chores. So they may be tired or exhausted. Under such circumstances, keeping the lines of communication will be lacking or where there is communication, it may be irregular. Communication is more than just talking. It is a two-way process of transmitting message(s), information or ideas which involve the sender(s) and the receiver(s) with resultant negative or positive action(s) and reaction(s).

When parents communicate with children, they should ensure that their communication is effective. It is unrealistic for parents to expect that the later years of children will be trouble-free and smooth just as the early years of childhood. Problems will definitely come, but clear, effective regular communication can be a key factor in preventing, reducing or solving them. Parents should have this in mind and be fully prepared by looking ahead and thinking ahead.

Many things are involved in establishing, building up and keeping family lines of communication working. Parents need to build up a depth of confidence, trust, good examples, mutual understanding and respect. Parents need to encourage natural expression from their children and emphasize the importance of politeness and courtesy as vital contributors to good communication.

Reproof will be necessary and should be given when needed with appropriate intensity. However, if children are habitually cut off, continually corrected when it is not necessary and even ridiculed by their parents when they speak, they will likely become withdrawn and prefer to discuss with outsiders. This may be risky. Parents need patience, appreciation and self-control to prevent this ugly situation from arising.

In understanding the needs of grown-up children, parents should recognize that their young adults or youth want more than ever, to be treated as individuals, they want guidelines and direction. This is due to the youth approach to eventual independence and the normal desire for wider latitude of movement and choice.

Furthermore, the ties with those beyond the family circle increase and strengthen. In positive response to this, parents should allow a degree of independence gradually increasing it as the children near complete adulthood, letting them make more and more personal decision under parental guidance and supervision. But a balance should be maintained in the restriction placed on the children and they should show that greater responsibility goes with greater freedom.

Parents truly have power and control over children and these can be re-enforced with knowledge and understanding. Failure to show understanding when correcting the children can lead to a breakdown of communication. Also make them feel that they are valuable members of the family, contributing to its welfare, even being allowed to share in some of the family's planning and decisions. Let the grown-up children know that by being diligent, serious and reliable workers always, they will gain self-respect and the respect and appreciation of others within and outside the family and throughout their dealings with people.

Parents cannot monitor the children completely throughout their lifetime. The children will surely come across different people (good and bad) in the society. So, parents need not express fear, instead they should build their household with wisdom, good moral code and right principles for guidance. This will motivate the children always to behave reasonably well.

Communicate with children in words and in actions. Moral values, discipline and reasonable behavior are far more likely to be instilled if there is a home atmosphere in which those principles are implemented. Have the attitudes you want your children to have. In the home, within the family circle, create a sound atmosphere for understanding, show love and forgiveness, allow a safe degree of freedom and independence, display justice and fairness, and let them experience a feeling of acceptance and belonging. In these ways, meaningful regular communication will exist within the family and manifest positively in the children.

CHAPTER 13

SEX EDUCATION

The regular communication discussed in the preceding chapter is a general type of talk among family members regardless of age. There are however, specialized talk directed particular to some crucial subjects which children must be instructed, particularly for those that have relative independence to socialize with people outside the family members. In other words, there must be frank talk on subjects such as sex education, drug addiction, alcohol, hair and dressing styles and so on.

Yes, frank talk is different from the routine family communication in that it involves honest and direct discussion which is presented in a way that other people might not like. For example, sex education is one of the commonest topics that many parents shy away from for various reasons well known to them. The directness of frank talk is such that names, functions, shapes, words descriptions of sensitive body parts, etc are discussed without any shame or feeling of embarrassment.

It is pertinent to note that the 'honesty and directness' involved in frank talk does not mean that regular family discussions are not based on honesty or sincerity. Therefore, instructing the children frankly, to an adequate extent on sexual matters and some other behavioral issues that could affect children adversely in their lifetime is not merely the right thing to do but it is a kind thing to do.

What is sex education?

WHAT IS SEX EDUCATION?

In general terms, sex is the physical activity by which people and animals can produce young by having sexual intercourse or mating with opposite sex (male or female) of their type. In terms of human being, sex is the Physical activity between a male person and a female person (couples) which include sexual intercourse. Education is the process of teaching, training and learning to improve knowledge and develop skills.

Sex education, therefore, is the subject of sexual activity and sexual relationship which is communicated through the process of teaching or training (primarily by parents) and learning (by children at different ages) about sex and sex-related matters with the aims of creating awareness, improving knowledge and developing good thinking about the benefits of proper sexual relationship and hazards of improper sexual relationship for male and female persons.

In accord with the definition of sex education above, it is the primary role of parents to start teaching this special subject as early as possible and regularly to their children at the proper level of understanding. If parents shy away or fail to teach their children, they will be taught poor, wrong, obscene and misleading lessons about sex and sex-related matters from improper sources.

Some sources of wrong and/or twisted information

include; friends, neighbors, television, internet, books, magazine and radio. It is vital to state that these sources are not condemned as bad but the manner some topics and subjects are discussed send wrong signals to children. On the part of children, they are expected to listen, speak out their minds, ask questions and accept this special education provided by their parents. Parents should not have the wrong view that sex education exposes children to immorality. It does not. In fact, home is the first and the best place to learn every detail about sex and sex education. Similarly, parents are the first and the best teacher to teach children about sex and sex education.

Sex education should not be as difficult as many parents imagine. As children grow, they become aware of their parts. At this stage, the children want to know the names of their body parts. Parents should be ready to tell them without skipping their sex organs and mention the correct names e.g. penis, vagina and breast just as you mention nose, eyes, mouth etc. In other words, teach the children in the proper context. As different stages are reached, parents should use the proper vocabulary and very simple and correct explanation.

For an in depth understanding of this subject, each parent may handle specific aspect of this subject. For example, the father can attend to the male children and masculine/puberty issues (e.g. sperm discharge and its implications) while the mother takes care of the female children and feminine/puberty issues (e.g. menstruation and its implications). However, combined teaching by both parents for all the children should never be ignored in a serious, respectful and frank manner. In a single parent family, the parent should teach all the children this vital subject with all seriousness.

When inculcating this teaching in their children, parents should emphasize the importance of reporting promptly anyone that attempt to sexually harass, entice, excite or fondle with any of their sensitive parts. This prompt response from the young children will prevent them from being raped or sexually abused.

In the case of teenagers and adult children, parents should let them know the regrettable consequences of pre-marital sex and misuse of their sexual organs. These include; unwanted pregnancy, sexually transmitted diseases, abortion, rearing of bastards, emotional problem, career destruction, permanent uterus damage and psychological problems to mention just a few. It could also lead to loss of life. The female children suffer the greater part of these bad outcomes. When proper and comprehensive sex education is provided, children will already be well aware of the changes to be expected. And when they hear other children discussing sex or sex-related matters, they will not be curious, unreasonably excited or eager to listen and perhaps practice the misleading information.

Prevention is always better than cure. Parents should therefore, continue teaching their children for as long as they live together. Even the grown-up children should be made to understand that they are not above guidance in this subject, because a male or female counterpart may be lured or enticed sexually for the perpetration of some evils or crimes with fatal consequences. Hence, the need for absolute prevention and caution is very important by avoiding distorted information, by listening to parents' training, by being self-disciplined and so forth.

The strategic roles parents should play include; monitoring their children's companions, the types of books children read, regularly and cleverly observe rooms, assess extra-curricular activities of children at home and schools, pay impromptu visits to school and hostels as well as their school teachers for behavioral and performance briefing and so on. It is a fact that parents cannot perfectly monitor their children throughout life, but parents' timely effort, good examples coupled with the children readiness to re-train themselves in their parents' positive direction and obedience will help a lot in achieving the lofty objectives of sex education.

CHAPTER 14

DRUG ADDICTION

Drug addiction can be defined as the intentional and habitual intake of very harmful substances in gaseous, liquid or solid form either by inhaling, smoking, chewing, swallowing or injecting through the veins thereby causing abnormal excitement, unconsciousness and other forms of adverse effects on the user.

Some of the common hard drugs include; marijuana, heroin, lysergic acid diethylamide (LAD) and cocaine to mention just a few. It is necessary to state that these hard drugs are completely different from tablets, capsules, caplets, tonic, powder or injection prescribed and or administered by medical personnel. These are normal medication used to treat patients and sick people. They are used based on doctor's prescriptions to prevent, cure or alleviate pains, illness or diseases.

It is compulsory for parents to discuss with their children on the proper use of prescribed medication, the hazards of hard drugs, the socio-economic effects of hard drugs on users and so on. Parents should monitor and observe their children regularly in addition to taking them out for occasional medical checkup. The whole family will benefit greatly if parents create time to attend public seminars and lectures organized by hospitals, pharmaceutical companies, government and non-governmental organizations. Family doctors can also offer very good counsels for the family.

Youth and grown-up children don't just wake up and become addicted to hard drugs. There are many reasons why some children are addicted to hard drugs. In some homes, the father or both parents are drug addicts. This opens an easy access for the children to try and master the dangerous act of drug abuse. Parent must not be drug addict. Parents must abstain from using hard drugs for them to teach their children properly on issues concerning hard drugs. Many children abuse drugs because of frustration, failure, disappointment, peer pressure, bad companions, personal problem and many other reasons. These reasons are not plausible and are not justified for any children to get involved in drug addiction. Some of the common effects of drug addiction are brain or psychiatric problem, violent actions and reactions, damage to organs and loss of life. Drug addiction can cause permanent family and relationship breakdown.

Finally, parents should carefully scrutinize their children's companions by using all possible strategies and tactics. Regular but frank communication in a relaxed atmosphere is also vital. Parent should always be alert when strange behaviors, strange feeling, irrational actions are observed in their children, particularly the male children.

CHAPTER 15

A BALANCED VIEW OF ALCOHOLIC DRINKS

Alcoholic drinks refer to any fermented liquids such as beer, alcoholic wine, ethanol, spirit and other alcohol-containing liquids that can make people drunk when it is consumed in excess or when an individual's personal limit is exceeded. An alcoholic is a habitual drinker of alcoholic beverages or alcoholic drinks. Alcohol is a derivative or product obtained from the processing or fermentation of some agricultural crops such as barley, rye, malt, grapes, orange, sugarcane, cassava and so on. Alcoholic drinks, therefore, are good and enjoyable consumable beverages only when used properly by adults.

In a family setting, parents need to show absolute caution and a balanced view in the use or consumption of alcoholic drinks. Before parents can train children effectively on how, when, where, and for what purpose alcohol should be used, they need to show a very good example either by drastically reducing their consumption of alcohol or by abstaining from it completely. Parents should emphasize that alcoholic drinks are meant for adults and it must be consumed responsibly. It is compulsory for pregnant women and nursing mothers to abstain completely from drinking alcoholic beverages. This will protect her life, her baby's and the life of the unborn baby (fetus).

If parents relax, care less or fail to inculcate discipline in this important subject, the children will learn it from wrong sources in a misleading way and practice it in the absence of their parents. In families where one or both parents are alcoholic, there will be disruptions in family peace. This will further manifest in form of anger, fear, nervousness, anxiety and lack of self-respect. It is important to note that children are at the receiving end in homes where the parents are alcoholic.

For example, some of the children may be assaulted physically, maltreated with severe injuries and even molested sexually. When these happened, the children's trust in the alcoholic parent(s) will shatter and they will not be able to communicate freely with the parent(s). This will eventually result in family and relationship breakdown. This will further results in a home devoid of peace and responsible children. Misuse of alcohol has many adverse health effects. What are some of the health hazards?

Parents who have the interest and love of their children at heart will emphasize the negative outcomes of alcohol abuse. These include; frequent sickness, mental confusion, unconsciousness, hallucination, organs (liver, kidney) damage and so forth. Furthermore, alcohol abuse can expose the user to many deadly health problems namely; cancer, heart and stomach diseases, diabetes, poor coordination, poor visual judgement, reduction in driving skills and untimely death. Economically, alcohol abuse is a waste of income and a job snatcher i.e. loss of employment.

Parents should let their children know that the use of alcohol is not the solution to frustration, stress, worries, failure, weakness and other personal problems. Instead, regular medical check-up, use of medication prescribed by doctors and counseling on personal health management from doctors are the solutions to these problems. Besides, self-discipline, self-determination contentment, self-control, adaptability will also be of benefits.

CHAPTER 16

DRESSING AND HAIR STYLES

In many homes, mothers determine and select the type of clothing materials, designs and styles that their young children wear, and also dress for the children. In the case, of hair styles, this responsibility is somehow shared in some homes. That is the father takes the male children to the barbing saloon while the mother attends to the hair style of the female children. This division of responsibility is common but it is not mandatory.

Since the parents introduce the young ones to patterns of dressing and hair styles, it is correct to say that the parents are responsible for what the children wear and their hairstyle. Therefore, it is logical to say that the moral principles and standards of the parents are reflected by what the children wear, how they wear it and their appearance as a whole.

This further shows the level of dress code permissiveness that parents will approve for the children when they grow up and eventually become adults. These children will continue with the pattern of dressing and hair style their parents always select for them and even do more in making either good or bad (decent or indecent) choices or selections. Although children need increasing freedom as they attain adult age, their personal choice is still a function of their upbringing by parents. In parallel with this, parents are primarily responsible for shaping the lifestyles of their children. What the parents sow is what they will reap.

Clothing materials and dressing styles specifically require parents to keep in mind some vital factors which include neatness, public perception and public appraisal of dressing, modesty and so on.

Some of the terrible consequences of imitating and dressing indecently particularly by female children include; rape and prostitution. It is possible for parents to enforce strict control if they always keep the vital factors mentioned above in mind.

Variety is the spice of life. If parents can afford to buy latest decent clothing materials for their children, it is good but if otherwise, the ones available should be made clean, and the children should be made to understand why they are unable to buy new clothing materials always. In other words, parents should always teach their children (especially the females) contentment.

Also of importance is the clothing materials used, how it is designed and how it is worn. All these presentations speak a lot about the person wearing it and the parents' view of moral values. Children with good moral values will put on good clothing materials well designed in a modest manner. What is modesty? Why do children need to be modest in their dressing?

Modesty is the awareness and operation within one's limitation. It is also personal purity, carefulness and judiciousness in mode of dressing. When children dress modestly, they express reverence for their parents and themselves, respect for the feeling of others and for their own conscience. Proper dressing should not be shocking to decency and should not be offensive.

Choice of hair styles should also be of concern to parents. Hair is the mass of natural thread-like outgrowth found commonly on the head at birth. These outgrowths are found in many areas of the body as growth continues and as a sign of maturity. Males and females are naturally endowed with hair. Most males have low hairs while females generally have long hairs.

Hairs may be straight, curly, locked or wavy in shape. Natural color of hairs include; black, pale gold (blonde) or golden white depending on individual genetic make-up. Geographical location and tribal origin also determine natural shapes of hair to some extent. The hairs on the head are natural coverings for both sexes. It enhances attractiveness and it is an indicator of old age for elders (when it changes to grey color).

Males are expected to have their hair styles either as clean shaved, low cut, moderately high with responsible look. Apart from occasional cultural requirements by some tribes e.g. for bereavement or health reasons, females choice of hair styles include; bunches, kolese, French plait, suku, braid, cornrows, bob, pigtails, cropped, layered and so on.

CHAPTER 17

PROSTITUTION

Prostitution is an indecent act of having sexual intercourse regularly mainly for money and/or benefits. A prostitute is any female person who regularly offers herself for sex in exchange for money or benefits.

For many years in the past, family name, sexual chastity and moral principles are treated with esteem. Today all these good moral reasonings are irrelevant for many youths and adults. Unlike males, the females are naturally endowed with sexually attractive body than their male counterparts. But these sexy body parts, romantic and sexual relationship must be mutually beneficial between legally married couples. That is between a husband and his wife only.

It is unfortunate that some females (youths and adults) chose to commercialize sex. The decision of these females to engage in prostitution raise some mind searching questions such as; why do some women chose a sexually immoral lifestyle? How did they get into prostitution? Are there alternatives to prostitution? What roles can parents play to prevent their female children from engaging in prostitution?

WHY ENGAGE IN PROSTITUTION?

Those involve in this sexually indecent practice give many reasons for choosing it as a profession or a habit.

Although some of these reasons may sound pitiable, they are in fact, not plausible, not tenable and therefore completely wrong to engage in prostitution.

Some of the reasons given by prostitutes include but not limited to the following: That their parents are aged and they have to support home expenses. That both parents are bereaved and they needed to earn income, that both parents have lost their jobs, that they are unable to secure a job after completing their education, that they needed money to sponsor their education, that they needed money to start a business. Furthermore, some shamelessly said; that they cannot cope with small salary jobs, that they are forced into it by friends, that they wanted to associate with the rich and the mighty in the society and that they engaged in it just to have fun and enjoy.

PROSTITUTES AND HAZARDS

Prostitutes are usually nocturnal sex workers found mainly in big cities, towns, eyebrow streets, offices, brothels, secondary and tertiary institutions, some guest houses, and some club houses. Those involved in this dirty job are young girls, teenagers, adults, divorcee and even some married women. Prostitutes usually hide their identity and other vital information depending on area and time of operation.

It is pertinent to state that prostitution is prone to many uncertainties, most of which have fatal consequences. For example, abortion, chronic sexually transmitted diseases

(STDs) are the commonest problems among prostitutes. Others are; cannibalization of parts and organs for rituals, excessive drugging, cold-blooded murder and bestiality to mention just a few.

ALTERNATIVES TO PROSTITUTION

There are many decent works women can do instead of engaging in prostitution. Some of the income- generating works include; hair dressing, tailoring, child care services, gardening, trading, catering services, fashion designing, work at home internet jobs and so on.

Sourcing funds or loans to start a small business may seem difficult or impossible, but it is not difficult because there are many options for individuals and cooperatives. Some of the reliable sources of small business funds include; micro-finance banks, non-governmental lending organizations, government small and medium enterprise firms, poverty reduction agencies to mention just a few.

PARENTAL RESPONSIBILITY

Prevention is always better than cure. The fact that prostitution is indecent and it usually ends with fatal consequence makes it necessary for parents to guide against it, by devoting sufficient time to discuss it in detail why the female children should not engage in prostitution and why the males should not patronize prostitutes. Where one or both parents are guilty of this immoral behavior, they must first wash themselves clean to be qualified in counseling their children. It is very important for mothers who engage in prostitution to stop it right away. Similarly, fathers who patronize prostitutes should stop it immediately. It is never too late to take this very urgent action, as further delay could bring calamity into the home, put an end to peace and happiness and eventually split the family.

Moreover, parents need to be loyal to each other, maintain chastity, be contented and display moral and material self-control. These vital qualities should be inculcated in children too. It is never too much to stress that females (particularly youths) are the actors involved in the immoral work called prostitution as they allow it to creep in to their heart as an easy means of making quick money or getting what they want.

Grown up children (especially the females) should be advised not to associate with indecent youths, not to succumb to peer pressure for indecent or immoral practices and to avoid all tempting factors or situation that could lead a male child to patronize prostitutes and a female child from engaging in prostitution.

CHAPTER 18

SELFISHNESS, GREED AND CORRUPTION

It is a natural tendency for children from infants to demand for more than what they require or what they need and attempt to claim ownership for almost everything that comes their way. They do this by different subtle methods such as crying incessantly, struggling with one another and even fighting to get what they want. It is not an overstatement to say that this ugly behavior spread like bush fires to adults, parents inclusive. No doubt, some of the driving forces behind this bad habits include; selfishness, greed and corruption. What is selfishness? What is greed? And what is corruption?

Selfishness is the habit of caring only about oneself rather than about other people. Selfish persons do not want to share things with other people. This habit is the same with self-interest, which is the habit of considering your own interest only and not caring about things that would help other people. Selfishness commonly originates within one person and is executed by that same person. This does not rule the possibility of it developing within a group of people and its being executed jointly. In other words, a group of persons can also come together to plan and work towards achieving a selfish objective or selfish objectives.

Greed is a strong desire for more wealth, power and so on. A greedy person always wants more than is necessary, fair or needed. This bad habit did not only follow a similar pattern with selfishness, it is more pronounced among people of high rank across all categories of professions. The self-employed are not left out. Greed is easily identified by an inordinate desire or wish to achieve an objective which in most cases is beyond reasonable and/or economic need.

When greedy persons want to achieve their objective(s), they either do it by denying people who actually needed it, or they prefer to acquire things illegally or in a dubious manner and avoid due process or they use their 'connection or link' in the society to achieve their greedy objectives. Many other methods are used by greedy people to achieve their goals and objectives. They do not care about other people's feelings or the adverse effects of their behavior on other people. The fact is that they want to achieve their objectives at all cost. Parent should avoid this bad habit and teach their children to avoid it too.

Corruption is a dishonesty and illegal behavior by people in positions of authority or power. It is the act of making somebody change from moral to immoral standard of behavior. A corrupt person is always willing to use his or her power to do dishonest or illegal things in return for money or to get an advantage. A corrupt person can also have a bad effect on somebody and make them behave in an immoral or dishonest way. In a similar manner to greed, corruption cuts across all categories of people, salary earners, self-employed, etc.

Corruption is a common behavior among the well-to-do

people in the society. Out of the three bad habits, corruption has the widest scope, covering local, national and international levels. Corruption is such a terrible behavior in that it uses blackmailing, kidnapping and assassination as some of its tools to achieve its objective. Corruption is the worst among these bad behaviors.

It is very important for parents to make necessary changes if they are involved in this bad habit. Parents should devote time to discuss this issue carefully with their family members and let them know the adverse effects of this bad behavior on people who practice it. Parents should also stress the need for their children to quit mixing or stop associating with people with these bad behaviors.

Some of the reasons why children must avoid all forms of corrupt practices include; keeping family name and personality clean, avoiding the wrath of law which include; long-term imprisonment, confiscation of illegally acquired property.

Finally, parents should inculcate good behaviors in their children. Some of these include; self-restraint, hardworking, modesty, honesty, contentment and so forth. No time is too small or too much to devote for regular discussion with children. Parents should not let the success, achievements, impressive performance or excessive freedom for children overshadow their reasoning in performing their parental roles. Parent should not be overly occupied by their business, work or search for money to the detriment of providing proper and qualitative training for their children. It is possible for parents to change the wrong view of many children who believe they can only make it through the illegal 'short cut' of corruption. Parents' success in this direction will present every child as a reference in the study of good conduct.

CHAPTER 19

CHOOSE GOOD COMPANIONS

Who is a good companion? A good companion or a good friend is that person who has similar feelings, opinions, interests and whose company you enjoy. A good friend is a male or female who shares in your work, pleasures and sadness. A good friend is someone who is helpful and supportive. A good friend is a person you know very well either of the same age, younger or older who may or may not be a relation or a family member. How can a child know who will be a good companion or a good friend? How can parents help their children to find wholesome associates?

Companions affect us profoundly. Youths in particular are susceptible to peers pressure. In most cases, children tend to be uncertain themselves and may at times feel overwhelmed by a desire to please and impress their associates. How vital it is that they choose good friends? As every parent knows, children will not always choose well because they are inexperienced; they need some guidance. It is not a matter of choosing their friends for them. Instead, as they grow, parents should teach them discernment and help them to see what qualities they should value in friends. Parents should teach them to love and respect those who possess honesty, humility, kindness, generosity, love, diligence and loyalty.

Let your children know that their friends are equally

your friends and that they should bring them home regularly for easy acquaintance, observation and interaction. This is very important because when undesirable changes are noticed in their behavior, dress, attitude, speech, etc, it will be easy to correct the wrong behavior in the children promptly and also advice their friends to be of good behavior.

It is normal and proper for children to know and have record of addresses and some other vital information of their friends. Similarly, parents must also have a copy of this record with them to ensure safety and security of their children. This will also help parents in searching for their children and their friends whenever there is need for this action.

Valuable friends are honest and seek each others' progress and success. The act of enticing or making friends by means of material possessions or money will not ensure good and reliable friendship. As soon as money or material possessions disappear, the friendship will stop. Good friends cannot be purchased. A child's choice of friend describes who the child is or who the child is likely to be.

In this day and age, parents cannot afford to be casual about their children associates. Do you know whom your children spend time with, whether face-to-face or otherwise? "Bad companions spoil useful habits." The importance of a child's choice of friend cannot be overemphasized. One friend of a child can either destroy or contribute positively to the good work parents have done.

Therefore, parents' roles involve more than simply shielding their children from bad influences.

Children need the right kind of friends. This is because in most cases, any person that is walking with wise persons will become wise and vice versa. Friendship is not limited to a child's age mate or contemporary. It is also important to teach children that they can make friends with older people. Association with exemplary seniors or elderly persons will give children the advantage of learning many good things and acquiring valuable experience.

Children cannot remain permanently friendless. Friendship can therefore, develop either because of compatibility of personality, family relationship, because of similar or the same religious belief, because of similar background or interest and so on.

In addition to the characteristics of a good friend discussed earlier, a good friend is a person who sticks closely with you, a person who is constant in his or her loyalty and friendliness, a person who comes to the aid of his companion in distress and gives counsel in truthfulness and faithfulness. Parents should always discuss issues concerning their children's friends and tactfully assess the type of friends or companions their children keep or associate with.

Finally, parents should not allow their children (particularly the adult) to live together with the opposite sex if they are not husband and wife. The reason why parents must not allow this is that this type of lifestyle have yielded many bad results both for the males and the females. Some of the bad and regrettable outcomes include; fornication, incest, disease transmission, unwanted pregnancy, abortion, giving birth to rejected or abandoned babies, having children out of wedlock, having malnourished babies, having maladjusted children, disruption of education, fight, emotional and psychological problems, stigmatization, court cases, forceful marriage alliance by parents and so forth.

CHAPTER 20

MAINTAIN A BALANCED VIEW OF RECREATION

Leisure time and wholesome, balanced recreation are necessary for the mind and body of a child to develop. When parents enjoy recreation with their children, family ties are strengthened and the children gain a sense of security.

Well chosen recreation is more than fun. It is a way for a child to learn and mature. Play is a natural part of a child's life. Parents must recognize this, while gradually introducing into the child's life an appreciation for work and a sense of responsibility. Recreation can be described as an activity that gives enjoyment or pleasure and contributes to happiness. Also, it is a particular activity that somebody does when they are not working either at home, in the neighborhood or far away from home.

In every family arrangement, the father is the head of the family and is responsible for providing for his household's needs in everything; including decent, healthy, harmless, non-violent recreation. However, a balanced view must be maintained always. Parents need to set a convenient balance for recreation by ensuring that whatever chores the child may come to have including academic homework are generally best done first; play comes second. In other words, there must be proper arrangement such that work time or programme do not conflict or clash with fun times. If possible, a flexible well prepared, combined programme may be designed.

Parents need to set time boundaries for their children to know how much is too much for recreation. Still on time balance for recreation, parents should not be overly occupied by their job such that it becomes difficult for them to spend time with their children and play with them. Therefore, parents should spend reasonable time not just for family discussions or other domestic activities but also in being true friends and companions for recreation. In this manner, excitement and happiness will flow freely in the family.

Another area which requires a balanced view of recreation is the type of recreation or the choice of recreation made by children. Parents need to teach their children how to judge what recreation is bad or harmful and what recreation is good. This will take time and effort. Children too, need to be obedient and be self-discipline.

Many recreation and entertainment programmes on the electronic media and public entertainment centers promote violence, crime and other demoralizing behaviors. The impression created when this type of entertainment are presented for public viewing is that they are enjoyable and acceptable. However, there are many pleasant and healthy recreations both at home and away from home. Some of these include; indoor games (e.g. scrabble, ludo, chess, card, draught, puzzles, etc), documentaries (e.g. nature, people, culture, place, technology, etc) on television and internet, outdoor sports, musical concerts and so on. When parents set a balanced view on type of recreation, there will be a big difference in a child's development. This is vital because it will help the adult children to differentiate, judge and choose a harmless recreation.

Additionally, a balanced recreation must be educative, entertaining and informative. It must also be morally, mentally, physically and emotionally up-lifting. These qualities differentiate decent recreation from indecent recreation and it will help children derive maximum enjoyment and satisfaction.

Recreation should not be indoors alone or within the family in the compound alone. Some interesting and healthy outdoor associations should be included. This will surely be beneficial to children because it will enable them develop a broadened understanding of people and places. But parents need to be cautious because when there is too much outside association or it is left uncontrolled, children will associate with bad people and imitate or emulate their bad behaviors, the family circle will become weakened or even fragmented.

Some other examples of wholesome recreation include; artwork, gardening, visits to zoological gardens, painting, visits to beach and museum, going for picnic, watching varieties of sports at stadium and sport centers and a host of other lively activities.

Social gathering can also be a rewarding form of recreation. When social gatherings are well supervised and not too large or too much time-consuming, it will contribute to a balanced development. Therefore, parents should properly guide and control recreation with a balanced view in mind. Children in turn, will learn that there is more to recreation than simply sitting passively and being entertained. The whole family should be involved in both passive and active non-violent, healthy entertainments and recreation.

CHAPTER 21

TEACH CHILDREN HOME MANAGEMENT

Parents have many duties to perform for their children. In addition to implementing the suggestions covered in the previous chapters, it is also important and compulsory for parents to provide specialized training for their adult children in home and family relationship management. Despite all difficulties faced by parents in raising children, it is the expectation and joy of parents to see their children as mature and responsible adults.

It is not an exaggeration to say that grown-up children are prospective husbands and wives. Hence, there is need for parents to provide this special training for their grown-up children. Some parents feel this subject is strange, abstract and impossible and therefore, it is not necessary. But the fact is that it is a crucial subject parents must train both male and female adult children.

When preparing adult children for this great task, parents must create time for regular discussions. This special training is not just an oral type like the usual regular family discussions. It is a combination of oral and practical training by the parents. It must include delegation of some parental duties, supervision, performance appraisals and control. It is important to state that many family members have been doing similar things at home casually or without paying special attention to its importance. The reason why this subject is specifically chosen is to create awareness and or inform parents on the need for special arrangement to groom their adult children in these special parental roles.

To succeed in this area, parent must practice and inculcate essential home management practices in their grown-up children. Besides, to complement home management, sound family relationship management virtues are necessary. These include flexibility and tolerance, team planning, love, respect, God-fearing attitude, care and consideration, endurance and contentment, support, empathy and forgiveness, cleanliness, thankful attitude, trustworthiness, equal treatment of in-laws, families and friends and so on. These family relationship management virtues will be treated in subsequent chapter.

HOME MANAGEMENT

Successful home management can be achieved when every family member supports the mother in this vital duty. The mother or the wife is the manager of home in a family. What is home management?

Home management is the process of effectively running a household. It is the process of **decision** making which also involves **planning, allocation, utilization, evaluation** and **controlling** the use of **available resources** of the family for the purpose of attaining or achieving family **goals**. Also home management is the proper management of the entire home affairs with the available resources to achieve family goals.

An ounce of prevention is better than loads of cure. If a home is well managed, it would save the family unnecessary costs and prevent huge future expenses on avoidable wants and dislike items. An example, of home management is taking care of children, providing good meals, making sure the house is clean, attending to the house needs and so on.

Provision of money for family needs is the natural responsibility of the husband. In a family where the husband or the father is the only one providing money, the wife or the mother should show understanding, maturity cooperative, and be supportive in addition to managing the money prudently.

Parents are required to apply the highlighted keywords in the definition provided above to achieve a resounding success in their home management practices. It is the duty of parents to inculcate this practicable approach in their children to serve as guide for them as they move closer to becoming parents in future.

Another crucial aspect of good home management is the environment or surroundings. Cleanliness is a pivotal factor in home management. If the house is tidy and clean but the surroundings are awful, the efforts of the parents may be in vain. This is because dirty environment exposes the entire family to health risks. It is the duty of every member of the family to ensure that the surrounding of the house is clean. Sound home management practices learned by the children from their parents will make them (male and female) versatile and be able to adapt or cope in any situation they find themselves.

Relationship management is another important area of special training parents must teach their grown-up children in preparing them for future parental roles. What are some of these virtues? How are they relevant to relationship management? What are the benefits of these virtues for the family?

CHAPTER 22

FAMILY RELATIONSHIP MANAGEMENT VIRTUES

Family relationship management virtues refer to the decent ways of behaving or good qualities expected of family members that will enable them live peacefully and happily with one another regardless of religion, tribes, culture, economic and national differences.

In order to enjoy and maintain good relationship, it is wrong to believe or assume that your spouse should know how you feel. This is because relationship can be complex and problems can manifest anytime.

Some of the family relationship management virtues include but not limited to; God-fearing attitude, love, flexibility and tolerance, acceptance of differences, team planning, sharing spirit, trustworthiness, negotiation, industry spirit, respect for individual, care and consideration, support, endurance and contentment, empathy and forgiveness, cleanliness, thankful attitude, equal treatment of in-laws and friends.

GOD-FEARING ATTITUDE

God-fearing attitude is one of the best virtues couples need to manifest to achieve an excellent result or succeed in the area of good relationship. This virtue means hating what is bad and doing what is good. If couples have this virtue; disagreements, problems and misunderstanding will reduce to minimum. This attitude is important in preventing couples from following a bad course and it helps in recognizing and avoiding injurious acts. Parents should inculcate this virtue in their children.

LOVE

Love is in the same category with God-fearing attitude. This is because when there is love between couples, both of them will try as much as possible to avoid offending each other. A person can be said to show love if he or she does not brag, not get puffed up, not boast on what has been achieved or what will be done. A loving person cares for others. He or she does not become provoked, shows concern for others, does not insist that everything be done in his or her own way alone, seeks the advantage of the others, does not look for an occasion or an excuse for provocation, not moved to outburst of anger, not easily offended by what others say or do, does not suspect or disbelieve others unless there was absolute proof. All parents should inculcate this virtue in their children.

FLEXIBILITY AND TOLERANCE

Couples should show flexibility. That is they should be able to adjust to suit new condition or situation of each other. Rigidity will hinder progress while flexibility will hasten progress. Similarly, couples should show tolerance for each other's opinion or behavior as the case may be. Flexibility and tolerance should be exercised reasonably. Flexibility and tolerance is needed among couples because both of them are two different people with different attributes. This difference can be blended, if both are flexible and tolerate each other in their actions. Children must learn from this good virtue.

ACCEPTANCE OF DIFFERENCES

Couples should be ready to embrace differences within a relationship rather than attempting to change the other person to be the same as ourselves. Changing the behavior of a person completely is not an easy thing to do. In fact, it is not possible in most cases. Rather than attempting to do this, couples should try to embrace their differences amicably with a view to achieving family goals and let their children learn from this.

TEAM PLANNING

Team planning is essential between couples to succeed in having good relationship. Some husbands find it difficult or think it is not necessary to plan home affairs with their wives. These husbands believe providing the regular house allowance for family needs will perform all the 'magic' in the family, including good relationship. This is not possible. Husbands should take the initiative for team planning. The wife should not see this arrangement as an avenue to disrespect or humiliate her husband's headship role. Team planning will ensure smooth and orderly running of the house. Team planning will build or improve good relationship between couples because both of them (particularly the husband) will be willing to discuss with each other before making decision.

TRUSTWORTHINESS

Distrust can cause great emotional harm, hinder good relationship and even split marriage. Conversely, trust will build confidence, soothe emotion, enhance happiness, build good relationship and solidify marriage bond. A trustworthy husband or wife can be relied on to do good, be honest, be sincere and avoid deceit. Couples must be concerned about each other's feelings and avoid tempting actions or thoughts that may destroy their marriage. Therefore, one of the bases of a successful marriage which will also build or enhance good relationship is trustworthiness.

MANIFEST INDUSTRY SPIRIT

The type of relationship between some couples is that of housemaster-housemaid whereby the wife alone performs all housework while the husband gives instructions or enjoys himself in front of the television, on the couch or in a restaurant. In this situation, the husband thinks this is the right thing to do because; he is the head of the family, he is a man, he is the breadwinner or he is a rich man. This thinking is absolutely wrong.

Husband and wife are created to complement each other. This divine instruction must apply to all aspects of the couples' life. And this should manifest for the children to see and learn. When both husband and wife are industrious and they train their children this good virtue, neither of the couple will be burdened with domestic work. One advantage of this training is that couples' health will be protected, particularly when the wife is pregnant or when she is nursing a baby. Hardworking couples will therefore, see domestic work as a fun and not as a task.

BE READY TO NEGOTIATE

Couples should understand each other's wants and needs and continue to know more about these wants and needs. When couples learn to know or discover more about each other, they will have very little problem about satisfying or yielding to each other's request. In other words, if couples are ready or they are prepared to negotiate on their wants and needs, they will be able to work out a way to fulfill their different goals without one person having to compromise totally. This fine quality will strengthen good relationship. Children must be taught to behave in the same manner.

RESPECT AND HONOUR EACH OTHER

Any form of competitive behavior by the wife will lead to disrespect, disregard, quarreling and slow down progress. Similarly, if the wife is dishonored, she will be depressed, unhappy and feel worthless. A wife will show respect by being polite in behavior, supporting the husband's decisions, not manifesting competitive spirit, by showing deep regard for the husband's headship position and so on. Likewise, the husband needs to honor his wife by not taking her for granted, by being considerate, by being considerate, by not treating her as just anybody, by caring for her and so forth.

For example, it is not wrong for a wife to assist her husband financially or otherwise. But the wife should show humility, maturity and submissiveness. In turn, the husband should not see this as usurpation of his headship roles. Instead, the husband should show understanding, appreciation and even commend his wife for her loving, caring complementary roles.

Both couples should be sincere with each other. Mere formalistic or 'eye-service' (particularly in the presence of visitors or guests) respect and honor is deceptive, misleading and can be dangerous. Therefore, parents should show and stress the need for genuine respect and honor in marital relationship for their grown-up children. These good qualities will enhance good relationship.

I AM IMPERFECT

Nobody is above mistake. This common saying is always correct and it is a statement of the fact that every human being is imperfect and therefore, prone to making mistakes time and again. Acceptance of this inborn factor will motivate couples to have deep thought and reasoned assessment of each other's behavior. However, there is a caution here. Parents should avoid abusing or misusing this factor (imperfection) as an instrument to cover avoidable mistakes or intentional wrongdoing.

SHOW CARE AND CONSIDERATION

Husband and wife need to care for each other. Care and consideration are twin qualities that operate together. Care involves providing for each others' needs within affordable range, giving genuine attention or thought to each other, expressing a feeling of importance or worth for each other and so on. Similarly, consideration involves thinking carefully about each other when planning or making decisions. It is also the quality of being sensitive towards each other and thinking about each other's wishes and feelings.

One of the pre-requisites of care and consideration for couples is manifestation of an unselfish attitude. We are in a world where selfishness is rampant. For a person to care and consider another, he or she must be unselfish. Parents therefore, need to be awake and train their children the benefits of these fine qualities.

ENDURANCE AND CONTENTMENT

Endurance is the ability to continue doing or bearing something difficult or unpleasant for a long period of time without complaining. It is the ability to be patient for a long time despite difficulties without losing hope. Contentment is a feeling of happiness and satisfaction despite the problem being faced. Husbands and wives must show endurance and contentment.

One fact about life is that no condition is permanent, and the only permanent thing is change. Things may be smooth today, but tomorrow it may be rough. No matter the depth of love, enjoyment and happiness between couples, there will be occasional changes that require endurance and contentment by one or both couples.

For example, economic hardships, disagreements and some internal or external man-made or natural issues and uncertainties may adversely affect the lifestyles and relationship between couples. This is a trying time for couples, but they should not allow it to develop hostility, buck-passing or malice because it may degenerate into separation or divorce. Parents should let their adult children know that it is not only how well a marriage relationship started that matter but also their ability to endure and be contented during difficult periods.

SHOW THANKFUL ATTITUDE

Words, comments or expressions of appreciation have since disappeared among many couples. This simple but important expression which is known as thankful attitude has been observed to enhance truelove, satisfaction, sense of worth and encouragement. To be thankful means to be pleased about something good that has happened or something bad that did not happen. It is an expression or comment which shows that you are grateful to somebody for something they have done. It is equally a polite way of accepting an offer.

Some thankful expressions expected among couples include; thank you my dear, I am very grateful, thank you honey, accept my thanks, thank you sweetie, well done my dear, I appreciate your efforts and so on. It is not too much to further hug or kiss each other as an extension of deep appreciation for each other's good deeds. Timely commendation is always refreshing and stimulating. It is an assurance for a wife that her husband appreciates her contribution and loving care and that he does not take her for granted. Wives too, must commend their husbands. All children must learn to be thankful no matter how small they benefit. Therefore, always practice and teach your children thankful attitude. It helps in building and or maintaining good relationship.

SHOW EMPATHY AND FORGIVENESS

It is possible for couples to understand each other's feelings, actions and reactions to a great extent. This is true if the couples have similar or identical experience in the past. This can also be true if couples possessed and applied empathy reasonably. Empathy is the ability to place yourself in your spouse's position. Application of empathy by couples is a sign of good reasoning and sound judgement.

Forgiveness is the act of stopping to feel angry with somebody who has done something to harm, annoy or upset you. Empathy and forgiveness are very important for couples because disagreements, misunderstandings and mistakes cannot be avoided completely.

If a husband or a wife has done wrong, they must be

ready to admit their mistake or wrongdoing and apologize sincerely without delay. This aspect is very vital as minor contrasting issues or problems may 'grow' and eventually explode, leading to fight, domestic violence, separation or break up in their marriage. Therefore, it is necessary to resolve differences calmly, amicably, maturely and promptly. It is not too much to be humble and make apologetic statements such as; I am very sorry, kindly forgive me, I have forgiven you, accept my apology and so on. This fine virtue will enhance marriage bond and relationship and couples will derive pleasure in each other's company.

TREAT IN-LAWS, FAMILIES AND FRIENDS POLITELY

In-laws refer to the parents of married couples, their immediate and extended families and relations of the couples. There is an erroneous belief by some people that the husband's relations are more important than the wife's or vice versa. Neither of these beliefs is correct. The two parents, their families and their relations are very precious, very important and should be treated in the same polite manner by the married couples.

Partiality towards some in-laws, families or relations against the others should not be practiced by couples. The type of family system (nuclear or extended) practiced should not be used in treating the in-laws, families and relations impolitely and disrespectfully. Also, status, level of education, age, wealth and other factors should not be barrier in treating them politely.

This subject may sound strange but it is very vital and should be given proper attention. This is because it has caused serious problems in many homes that ignored its importance. For example, in homes where there is unequal or unfair treatment of in-laws, families and friends of the wife; envy, hatred, quarreling, disunity and suspicion between couples and family members and relations are very common. To avoid these problems, couples should treat in-laws, families and friends from both of them fairly, with unbiased mind, politely, and favorably regardless of any internal or external factors. The couples should see all these people as the same, one family and that none of them is superior to the other. Application of this positive thinking will result in a successful marriage with sound family relationship.

CHAPTER 23

CARE FOR AGEING PARENTS

In some countries, nuclear family system is practiced. Because of this, ageing parents do not live with their children. This depends on many different flexible factors from one country to the other. In these countries, the aged live in special residences (with all necessary facilities) called geriatric homes. The only thing these aged people miss is that they are not in the same residence with their children. Their children and grandchildren can visit them as often as they wish.

On the other hand, extended family system is practiced in many countries. In countries where this system is practiced, aged parents live with any of their adult children until they passed away.

It is compulsory for children to care for their aged parents regardless of the type of family system practiced. Aged parents require this care because of their frequent old age health problems, lack of strength and so on. This is the way in which children can show appreciation for their parents' many years of parental care in terms of loving attention, their hard work, self-sacrifice, anxious care, expenses and risks-taking to mention just a few.

Some children either willingly or unwillingly do not have time for their aged parents. Children owe their life to their parents. Therefore, there are no justifiable reasons for them not to take care of their aged parents. It is because of the noticeable uncaring attitude of some capable (in cash and/or in kind) adult children that informed the discussion on the need for children to care for their aged parents. In other words, some adult children have the resources to take care of their aged parents but they deliberately decided not to do so. What are some of the signs of old age? In what different ways can capable adult children care for their aged parents?

SIGNS OF OLD AGE

As parents grow old, various degrees of signs become obvious, so they require more and more attention from their adult children. Parents can be said to be ageing when there are noticeable health deterioration which frequently interfere with their normal activities. This decline in health condition may be internal, external or combination of the two. Children should always be alert and attend promptly to their ageing parents. They should not wait till things get out of hand. What are some of the signs of old age?

Some of the signs of old age include changing of black or dark hair to white or grey, aided movement, wrinkled body, poor sight, loose teeth, recurring sickness, physical disabilities, trembling hands, rapid loss of strength, health problem complications and so on.

Other indicators of ageing include; failing memory. This sign makes it difficult for them to remember many of their normal or routine activities. For example, they forget times, days, seasons and appointments easily. Some of the ageing parents behave just like small children. Difficulty in sleeping, sleeplessness, frequent complaints and a host of other signs or symptoms are noticeable in ageing parents. The types of symptoms or signs in ageing parents vary, and these depend on many past and present factors. When parents are ageing, what different types of care or attention should they be given?

TYPES OF CARE FOR AGEING PARENTS

Foremost a among the attention that must be given to ageing parents are; provision of good balanced meals, regular and prompt attention to their health (medical care) and hygiene (particularly their house, surroundings and the materials they use). Besides this basic care, it is important to care for them materially, emotionally, spiritually and also keep them active.

Caring for ageing parents materially depends on the children financial capability. However, parents can be given the honor and respect of making a choice within the financial limits of their children. Some of the material needs of ageing parents include clothing, simple shoes, jewellery, flowers, toys, indoor games items and so on.

Emotional needs can be provided by letting them feel loved, respected, needed and be treated as valued members of the family without any form of discrimination or isolation. Some of the effects of emotional care include; happiness. Also, they will not feel hopeless and they may live longer. If parents live in geriatric homes, they can still be cared for emotionally by visiting them regularly to play and chat with them, by making regular phone calls, by contacting them on the internet, by sending short letters and gifts to them, by sending recorded music, stories, or films to them and so on. Also, parties can be organized for them. These and even more will keep them emotionally active and happy.

Just as material and emotional care are necessary to ageing parents, spiritual attention is equally vital for them. Some parents are so devoted to their religion such that they hardly move around without their Bible, Quran and or other worshiping symbols and publications. Ageing parents can be cared for spiritually by providing them with these worshiping items and publications. Also, religious seminars, lectures or sermons can be organized for them.

MAKE AGEING PERIOD LIVELY FOR PARENTS

Apart from the usual care and attention that must be provided for ageing parents by their children, the years of ageing can be made very lively and interesting for parents in many ways. Unfortunately, the twilight period of many aged parents is so dull and passive to the extent that they would prefer to die instead of living. It is a good idea to engage aged parents in variety of activities that is commensurate with their strength and capability.

Some of the wholesome activities that children can engage their ageing parents include but not limited to the following: taking them out for picnic, taking them out to zoological garden, swimming pool, museum, beach, sport centers, film or theater house and some other places of entertainment. Aged parents can also be taken out for a stroll in the neighborhood, can be invited to participate in cooking and some other lively exercises in and around the house.

Besides, regular communication with ageing parents is beneficial both for their brain, mouth and jaws. They can be asked to narrate some of their past experiences or tell stories. Children can also involve their ageing parents in indoor board games. Handicrafts such as knitting work to make baby's sweaters, shawls, caps, socks and gloves from wool and cotton threads will prevent their hands from getting stiff and keep their blood veins and muscles active.

BENEFITS OF CARING FOR AGEING PARENTS

Adult children do not care or attend to the needs of their ageing parents because of what they will gain or what they will benefit from them. It is a divine responsibility that the children must perform. But while fulfilling this divine responsibility, children indirectly derive valuable benefits. One of the main benefits of caring for ageing parents is the acquisition of priceless experiences during their interaction with them. Apart from this, children who cared for their ageing parents will be able to develop essential qualities namely love, self-sacrificing spirit, endurance, sharing spirit, diligence, humility and tenderness to mention just a few.

In addition, when children care for their ageing parents without discrimination, happiness will be enhanced in the family. Spirit of giving will be stimulated in the family due to their generous attitudes for their ageing parents. Emotional feelings of the ageing parents can be understood and this in turn, will enhance the emotional perception of the entire family. Above all, the children who cared for their ageing parents will experience great achievement and satisfaction for performing a divinely assigned responsibility to care for their ageing parents.

SUMMARY

Imagine a world where family values and glory will be restored. Imagine a world where the parents and the children will live together in peace, in harmony, with love and the children grow up to become responsible parents in the society. This was the situation of families many decades of years ago. Obviously, this is the desire of all parents/families nowadays. But unfortunately they are unable to achieve it. Why is it so? What is the trend in the family situation nowadays? This handbook contains practical lasting solution for parents and for prospective couples to help them succeed in their marriage and family relationship.

Nowadays the situation of the family is awful. Family breakdown is rampant globally for many untenable reasons and/or for many avoidable mistakes. For most of the reasons and mistakes, parents cannot be freed. But unfortunately, children are always at the receiving end. They bear the brunt. And still continue to reap the rotten fruit (bastards, rapists, robbers, prostitutes, kidnappers, drug addicts, etc.) of parental failures worldwide. What steps can parents take to revive the lost peaceful and happy family years? What roles should the children play?

This handbook highlighted on the family situation in the past, compared it with the present situation in the family and proffers practical corrective answers that will bring the family back on track.

In view of parents' desire for a successful family, this book discusses the two periods in family life. These are the pre-marital and the marital periods. The pre-marital period focuses on what prospective couples (a man and a woman) must do (requirements) to set up a solid foundation for a successful, peaceful and happy family. The marital period covers the parenthood life. In other words, what the parents must do in terms of planning for their family and implementing the family plan to accomplish their roles which include but not limited to home training, education, and caring for the general well being of the family.

www.ingramcontent.com/pod-product-compliance
Lightning Source LLC
Chambersburg PA
CBHW051945160426
43198CB00013B/2306